Virtue as Consent to Being

 McMaster Divinity College Press
McMaster Ministry Studies Series

When Storms Come: A Christian Look at Job (2010)
by Thomas Edward Dow

Virtue as Consent to Being
A Pastoral-Theological Perspective on Jonathan Edwards's Construct of Virtue

PHIL C. ZYLLA

☙PICKWICK *Publications* • Eugene, Oregon

VIRTUE AS CONSENT TO BEING
A Pastoral-Theological Perspective on Jonathan Edwards's Construct of Virtue

McMaster Ministry Study Series 2

Copyright © 2011 Phil C. Zylla. All rights reserved. Except for brief quotations in critical publications or reviews, no part of this book may be reproduced in any manner without prior written permission from the publisher. Write: Permissions, Wipf and Stock Publishers, 199 W. 8th Ave., Suite 3, Eugene, OR 97401.

Scripture quotations taken from the New American Standard Bible.® Copyright © 1960, 1962, 1963, 1968, 1971, 1972, 1973, 1975, 1977, 1995, by the Lockman Foundation. Used by permission. (www.Lockman.org)

McMaster Divinity College Press
1280 Main Street West
Hamilton, Ontario, Canada
L8S 4K1

Pickwick Publications
An Imprint of Wipf and Stock Publishers
199 W. 8th Ave., Suite 3
Eugene, OR 97401

www.wipfandstock.com

ISBN 13: 978-1-60899-504-2

Cataloging-in-Publication data:

Zylla, Phil.

    Virtue as consent to being : a pastoral-theological perspective on Jonathan Edwards's construct of virtue / Phil C. Zylla.

    vi + 158 p. ; 23 cm. Includes bibliographical references and index.

    McMaster Ministry Study Series 2

    ISBN 13: 978-1-60899-504-2

    1. Edwards, Jonathan, 1703–1758. 2. Christian ethics — History — 18th century. 3. Virtue. I. Title. II. Series.

BJ1224 Z9 2011

Manufactured in the U.S.A.

Contents

Pati Cum / vi

Introduction / 1

1 Reflections on the Pastoral Life of Jonathan Edwards / 9

2 Virtue Theory and Edwards's Concept of True Virtue / 45

3 The Language of Moral Vision / 75

4 A Constructive Proposal: Virtue and Pastoral Theology / 103

Appendix A: Key Events in the Life of Jonathan Edwards / 129

Appendix B: Significant Writings of Jonathan Edwards / 130

Appendix C: The Seven Days of Virtue / 131

Bibliography / 147

Suggestions for Further Reading / 153

Index of Authors / 157

Pati Cum

with you I suffer
the strange solidarity
of affliction

with you I wait
for the grace to move
toward hope

with you I suffer
the long anguish
of eternal night
and silent screams

with you I strain
for a glimpse
of a day
normal

with you I walk
though my legs
refuse to move
and see
though my eyes
refuse to open

with you I sing
the song
and laugh
the laugh
and suffer
the suffering

. . . pati cum

—Phil C. Zylla

Introduction

It might seem unlikely that a book on virtue would have much relevance to the issues confronting our broken world. While many still think of virtue in moralistic terms, the idea of a moral philosophy founded on a theoretical conception of virtue has been gaining ground in recent scholarship. With this renewed interest in virtue come questions concerning the nature of the moral life in general and the ways in which we will respond to the growing sense of despair with regards to the complex problems in our world. At the heart of this book is the investigation of the compelling features of moral vision. It is my contention that moral vision is not only the result of debunking morally numbing myths, but also demands that we advocate a constructive vision of virtue.

Resurgence of advanced thought on the theme of virtue has been evident in the past decade in a variety of academic disciplines. This book seeks to modify and advance Jonathan Edwards's concept of virtue as "consent to being" by offering the pastoral theological notion of virtue as a relational dynamic of "suffering with." The project enters the current dialogue by regarding the concept of virtue from the unique perspective of pastoral theology.

Research concerning the nature of the moral life, and especially central issues of moral formation, are intrinsic to the interests of pastoral theology. While contributions on the theme of virtue have been rather limited within the field, it is my contention that pastoral theology offers a unique perspective and significant voice to the current debates. The introduction of Edwards's construct of virtue as "consent to being" is offered as an important theological addition to the growing body of academic literature on the theme of virtue.

The idea of virtue as "consent to being" was conceived by the eighteenth-century pastor and theologian Jonathan Edwards (1703–1758) in a dissertation entitled *The Nature of True Virtue*, published posthumously in 1765.[1] This attempt to articulate the concept of the moral life within his greater theological system was written near the end of his life, and represents the mature thought of a keen theological mind. Drawing from the epistemology of John Locke, Edwards conceived a construct of virtue that is relevant to the modern debates concerning the moral life. I will draw out the implications of Edwards's virtue theory and expand his views toward a more dynamic conception of virtue for pastoral theology. It is my contention that Edwards's vision of the moral life was deeply affected by his own pastoral experiences and that a pastoral theology of virtue will reflect on these experiences as part of the interpretive framework offered. The core concept of virtue as "consent to being" will be developed from a pastoral theological perspective. I believe that Jonathan Edwards's construct of virtue can make a significant contribution to pastoral theology if it is expanded to include the experience of suffering and the pastoral response of compassion.

PASTORAL THEOLOGY AND VIRTUE

Through engaging the current discussions about virtue in moral philosophy and ethics with Edwards's philosophical theology, the concept of virtue is both altered and enriched. While some still consider the idea of virtue to be an outmoded conception of the moral life, many are advocating a renewal of virtue theory as one way out of what Gilbert Meilaender calls "a widespread dissatisfaction with an understanding of the moral life which focuses primarily on duties, obligations, troubling moral dilemmas, and borderline cases."[2] Here I summarize and explore the concept of virtue in theological ethics and moral philosophy for its connections with Edwards's idea of virtue. This effort provides the necessary framework from which to offer a theoretical understanding of virtue from the perspective of pastoral theology.

In order for pastoral theology to contribute a voice to these important discussions in virtue theory, a specific method must be considered. T. W. Jennings offers the perspective that pastoral theology matures through critical reflection and dialogue. If such dialogue is to be helpful it should "be directed toward a common subject matter," and the serious-

---

1. A recent edition of *The Nature of True Virtue* is included in Ramsey, ed., *Ethical Writings*.

2. Meilaender, *Theory and Practice*, 4.

ness and fruitfulness of such dialogue may be tested by "whether the conceptuality and vocabulary of both sides is altered and enriched through the process."[3] Jennings asserts that "the sign of a mature, responsible, and fruitful dialogue is that both sides come to require revision in the light of the discussion."[4]

This book extends the dialogue about virtue by contributing a specific idea of the construct of virtue from the unique perspective of pastoral theology. Such an effort requires an examination of the literature on the nature of virtue currently in vogue in the fields of moral philosophy and ethics. It requires also the construction of a pastoral theological framework from which to enter the discussion about virtue. I trust that my book will bring this new voice into the dialogue in a manner that will both alter and enrich our understanding.

JONATHAN EDWARDS'S CONSTRUCT OF VIRTUE

I have chosen to use the construct of virtue developed by the Puritan pastor and theologian Jonathan Edwards for two primary reasons. First, rather than relying on definitions derived from Aristotle or Aquinas, Edwards offers a concise definition of virtue. One of his crowning achievements was that he was able to articulate a clear conception of virtue. His proposal that virtue is "consent to being" may be seen as both an advanced philosophical conclusion and an important pastoral theological construct. One of my aims is to bring this fresh definition of virtue into the current discussions in order to advance the notion of virtue from a theological perspective.

Second, Edwards adds a particularly pastoral theological construct to discussions about virtue. Pastoral theology is a particular type of contextual theology. It is "a form of theological reflection in which pastoral experience serves as a context for the critical development of basic theological understanding."[5] The pastoral perspective of Edwards's theology is significant. While few would readily consider Edwards a pastoral theologian, he clearly developed his theological reflections from the vantage point of his life work as minister of Northampton parish. While seriously engaging the philosophical questions of his day and entering into the

---

3. Jennings, "Pastoral Theological Methodology," 864.
4. Ibid.
5. Burck and Hunter, "Protestant Pastoral Theology," 867.

theological debates of eighteenth-century New England, Edwards must be understood primarily as a pastor. I contend that his idea of virtue adds a new and important pastoral theological voice to the discussions about virtue that continue to unfold in moral philosophy and ethics.

However, this voice must be critically examined in order to plumb its usefulness for the postmodern era. I use Edwards's idea of virtue as a foundation for a pastoral theological construct of virtue, but also move beyond it by introducing the dynamics of suffering and compassion into the fabric of virtue theory. It is my contention that pastoral theology offers a depth dimension or grounded voice to the current debates about virtue. Hence, while dependent on Edwards's construct of virtue as "consent to being," I propose an understanding of virtue that is more dynamic and that specifically addresses the common experience of suffering and the pastoral response of compassion.

At the heart of research on virtue lies an unsettling difficulty in this respect. Attention to the ethical construct of virtue tends to minimize the common experience of suffering. While ethical theories of virtue probe the moral complexities that suffering produces, they often fail to enter into the experience of suffering itself as a vital component of the theory. While seeking to understand the nature of virtue, theorists in moral philosophy and ethics often fail to connect such theoretical discussions with the very life of brokenness that we all experience in this world. Such reflection, though helpful, has the effect of an autopsy; it is as though we are probing something dead. I contend that a mature theory of virtue will probe the mystery of suffering and enter into the pain of that suffering as a vital connection with the expressed vision of the good. Pastoral theology engages the concept of virtue precisely in this way.

PASTORAL THEOLOGY AND THE PRIORITY OF COMPASSION

From the perspective of pastoral theology, the notion of virtue includes an attentiveness to the dynamics of participation in a broken world. Pastoral theology has always been interested in the ideas of care and compassion. The current debates about virtue are of vital interest to pastoral theology, which, as a discipline, has an on-going interest in the issues of moral formation and character development. In my opinion, much of the literature on virtue fails to acknowledge the dynamic of suffering. Recognizing that dynamic may be one of the important contributions to virtue theory from the perspective of pastoral theology. In particular, I offer an expanded view of Edwards's construct of virtue as "consent to being" that regards compassion as a central or guiding motif.

At the heart of all pastoral action is the deeply rooted comprehension of the reality of suffering. Pastors and chaplains risk involvement in the stranglehold of a universe gone awry with the hope of helping and of alleviating some anguish. Early pioneers in the field of pastoral theology, such as Anton Boisen, Seward Hiltner, and Wayne Oates, worked to unearth the deep dimensions of anguishing experiences in order to bring the light of hope to bear on even the most traumatic and tormenting forms of personal and social despair. Boisen articulated a guiding vision for the field of pastoral theology when he stated, "I am hoping and laboring for the day when the specialists in religion will be able with his help to go down to the depths of the grim abyss after those who are capable of responding, those in whom some better self is seeking to come to birth."[6] Such a perspective locates hope at the center of the pastoral theological enterprise.

A dynamic conception of virtue from the perspective of pastoral theology confronts the experience of suffering and moves toward the stance of hope. In order to understand this, we must explore the deeper notion of compassion, which comes from the Latin, *pati* "to suffer" and *cum* "with." Virtue as "consent to being" will be developed in an expansive way to include the significant pastoral response of compassion.

PLAN OF THE WORK

The first chapter draws out the context within which Jonathan Edwards developed his vision for the moral life, and looks for interpretive clues to Edwards's moral thought in the specific nuances of his life journey. In order to appreciate Edwards's conception of virtue we must understand his life from the perspective of his chosen vocation as a minister and the various challenges he faced in the parish. Edwards failed to appropriate his moral vision in the context of his own pastoral work; it was not, in fact, until after his expulsion from the Northampton parish and his experience of becoming "worldless" that he was fully able to express his theological construct of virtue. These insights form an important

---

6. Boisen, "Distinctive Task," 12.

background to the argument built on the foundation of Edwards's moral thought and an advanced conception of true virtue.

The second chapter engages the current discussions about virtue from moral philosophy and ethics with Edwards's conception of virtue as "consent to being." While some may question the usefulness of Edwards's ethical construct for the current debates, there are good reasons for considering Edwards's contribution to be an advancement of the general discussions about virtue. At the heart of this chapter is an explanation of some of the important nuances in Edwards's conception of virtue. The chapter concludes with a description of the usefulness of his concept in moral philosophy generally and toward the development of a pastoral theology of virtue in particular.

Chapter 3 is a transitional discussion concerning the nature of language as a way to express and mediate the concept of moral vision in the development of a theoretical construct of virtue for pastoral theology. This book argues throughout that the experience of suffering is an important link to a mature moral vision and a subsequent pastoral theology of virtue. This chapter advances this perspective by offering specific proposals concerning the use of "experience-near" language and explanations of the fabric of moral vision itself. Three specific proposals are offered. The first is that moral insight is the product of reframing or reforming the moral dimensions of the suffering moment. The second proposal is that a sense of personal history that integrates the moral vision for the good and the experiences of suffering can be captured in the form of a moral quest. The third assertion is that mature moral vision must go beyond the debunking of morally numbing myths to offer constructive proposals about how to live (the life of virtue).

The final chapter is a constructive proposal for pastoral theology that advances the notion of virtue to include compassion as an integrative motif for a pastoral theological construct. In an effort to explicate this understanding of pastoral theology a descriptive proposal is used as the framework from which a dynamic interpretation of the nature of virtue as consent to being can be developed. Such a conception of virtue goes beyond those approaches to pastoral theology that would view it simply as a framework from which to work out an ethic of virtue. This proposal has been frequently suggested in approaches to pastoral theology and ethics. However, I propose to go beyond such efforts to express a specific construct of virtue from a pastoral theological perspective. Although this is achieved only in a preliminary way, the evidence points to a dynamic conception of virtue as consent to being when the idea of compassion is integrated as the connecting tissue between the experience of suffering and the inward striving towards the greatest good. It is here, precisely, that I offer the expressed conception of virtue as "suffering with," which may, in the end, be a variation on the theme of Edwards's consent to being from the particular viewpoint of pastoral theology.

Whatever virtue is, clearly a pastoral theological approach to this concept will require a dynamic interpretation that goes beyond moralism and the application of ethical theory, and moves toward some concrete expression of the essence of virtue that attends at once to the suffering and hope of the human condition, one in which the pastoral theologian finds herself[7] on a moral quest for participation with those who suffer. Standing there, she may well discover that agreement and consent to suffering is the closest conception of virtue yet. This work proposes, therefore, to capture the idea of virtue as a relational and ontological dynamic that, from the perspective of pastoral theology, includes the experience of suffering and the response of compassion.

---

7. Contemporary scholarship has become sensitized to the importance of inclusive language and I share the conviction that all writing should reflect a vision that is inclusive of both genders in every respect. I have chosen to alternate between the masculine and feminine throughout this book in an even distribution. This allows the flow of thought to continue without the awkward use of he/she or the use of plural when the singular is more appropriate. I use he and she interchangeably, and the reader is encouraged to understand that both men and women are equally being considered in every case.

1

Reflections on the Pastoral Life of Jonathan Edwards

INTRODUCTION

Toward the end of his life, Puritan theologian Jonathan Edwards, in a dissertation entitled *The Nature of True Virtue*, expressed his idea of virtue as "consent to being in general." This important theological construct will be used throughout this book. In order to understand Edwards and to gain insight into his vision for ministry I will focus in this chapter on the life of Edwards the pastor, and look for clues to the origins and development of his vision for the moral life.

Edwards may seem a peculiar choice to offer us a modern vision for virtue in pastoral theology. Two factors guide the choice for the use of his conception of virtue in this work—the resurgence of virtue theory in modern theological ethics and Edwards's own pastoral framework.

In the past number of years there has been a resurgence of interest in the area of virtue theory, particularly in theological ethics and moral philosophy. However, reflection on Edwards's scholarly contribution in this area has been noticeably absent. Though recognized as one of the foremost theological thinkers of North American history, Edwards remains largely unexplored in regard to his concept of virtue. My intention here is to draw out his theological concept of virtue and to use it in the framing of a modern construct for pastoral theology.

Edwards's pastoral ministry took place in the eighteenth century and reflects the Puritan era of church life in New England. Edwards was, first and foremost, a pastor. He regarded the ministry of the parish to be his life-long calling. To understand his framework demands that we take seriously his work as a parish pastor. He did not do theological reflection outside of the community of faith, but was instrumental in the development of the Northampton parish through the years of what is termed "the Great Awakening." His use of the epistemology of John Locke, the scientific discoveries of Newton, and his own reflection on the important themes of Reformed theology combine in one of the most original and broad frameworks for theology ever developed in North America. His blend of philosophical reflection, theological articulation, and pastoral integration combine to produce an important aesthetic theology. Edwards scholar Sang Hyun Lee recognizes the magnitude of his thought for modern theology:

> What Edwards accomplished in the course of his search for a philosophical understanding of the Christian faith was a thoroughgoing metaphysical reconstruction, a reconception of the nature of reality itself. There is in Edwards' thought a shift of categories in terms of which the very nature of things is explicated.[1]

But Edwards's manner of being a pastor also requires critical assessment. From our perspective today his practice of ministry left much to be desired. Edwards was withdrawn from his congregation, often spending twelve to fourteen hours a day in his study. He was engaged in the theological debates of his day, but often in ways that seem naive regarding his own pastoral situation. He is not, therefore, being held up in this book as a model pastor. In fact, I believe he missed the significance of his own theological construct of virtue for his pastoral work. While extrapolating an important and vital concept of virtue, he was never quite able to bring this to bear on his own ministry in Northampton. By reflecting on these themes, we can plumb the richness of his ideas for modern pastoral theology in a way that is more integrative than was reflected in his own pastoral work.

In order to mine the resources of his important contribution on this topic it is necessary to be open to the complete mindset of Jonathan Edwards: his life, his vision for ministry as a parish pastor, and the development of his theology. I will move systematically through Edwards's life, paying close attention to look for clues to assist in understanding his theological idea of virtue in its final development in his dissertation *The Nature of True Virtue*.

---

1. Lee, *Philosophical Theology*, 3.

PERSONAL LIFE OF JONATHAN EDWARDS

Family Influences

Jonathan Edwards was born on October 5, 1703, in East Windsor, Connecticut. He lived for his first thirteen years in the parsonage there, as he was the son of the minister, Timothy Edwards. Jonathan learned the rudiments of ministry from observing his father in the East Windsor parish. His father studied at Harvard and was ordained in 1695 at East Windsor where he remained until his death. Among the lessons of the East Windsor parish were struggles over salary, ministerial authority, and the need for building a new church, all three of which became significant in Edwards's later ministry in Northampton.

Edwards was also witness to genuine "reviving of religion" in the East Windsor congregation. In such times nominal Christians became fully convinced of their need for Christ and many turned toward God with utmost seriousness. Later in his life he would write:

> The remarkable pouring out of the Spirit of God, which thus extended from one end to the other of this country, was not confined to it, but many places in Connecticut have partaken of the same mercy ... in East Windsor, my honored father's parish, which has in times past been a place favored with mercies of this nature ... there having been four or five seasons of the pouring out of the Spirit to the general awakening of the people there since my father's settlement there.[2]

As the "Great Awakening" broke out in 1734–1735 and again from 1740 to 1742 in New England, Edwards would have had many occasions to reflect on his boyhood observations regarding his father's parish. No doubt these impressions greatly affected his perceptions of authentic spirituality, which he would later write about in his famous work, *The Religious Affections*, published in 1746.[3]

Edwards's lineage was not notable on his father's side but his mother was Esther Stoddard, daughter of Solomon Stoddard, the eminent pastor of the Northampton parish since 1669. The Stoddard family was highly respected throughout New England. By the time of Edwards's birth,

---

2. Edwards, "Faithful Narrative," 349.
3. See Appendix A for an outline of Edwards's writings and key events in his life.

Northampton parish had become "the largest in inland Massachusetts and its pulpit one of the most influential in the whole colony."[4]

In years to come Edwards would become Solomon Stoddard's successor, a fact that would cause him some turmoil. That he respected his grandfather is clear from correspondence at the end of his ministry in Northampton. He writes, "My grandfather, [was] a very great man, of strong powers of mind, of great grace and great authority, of a masterly countenance, speech, and behavior."[5] Nevertheless, he was also keenly aware of how his grandfather's position on the subject of communion became his demise. He writes in the same letter, "Mr. Stoddard, though an eminently holy man, was naturally of a dogmatical temper; and the people being brought up under him, were naturally led to imitate him."[6]

His conceptions of ministry, then, were worked out in the context of the East Windsor parish and under the shadow of the influential and eminent pastor, Solomon Stoddard. In some ways these factors hindered him from the freedom to develop his own course of action in pastoral work. His private theological views did not always coincide with his public approach to ministry. Had he been able to work out a pastoral theology from his own theological framework, it might have looked much different.

It is important to recognize the significance of Edwards's life situation for the development of his ethical thought, particularly for his idea of virtue. He would have recognized his responsibility to carry the faith forward in the tradition of his father and in keeping with the teaching of divinity taken at Yale College. This responsibility would increase as he came to terms with his role as the successor of his venerable grandfather. It may be very significant, in the end, to recognize that his dissertation on virtue was written in the period of his life when he was free from this role of defender of Puritan theology and was no longer working in the shadow of Solomon Stoddard. It was in the context of this freedom that Edwards was to articulate his most important conception of virtue.

---

4. Murray, *Jonathan Edwards*, 6.
5. Edwards, "Memoirs," cxxxi.
6. Ibid.

Yale College

As noted, Edwards was educated at Yale College. At the time, the college was still young and its permanent location not yet decided. He was listed as a freshman at the college in Connecticut on September 12, 1716, when he was only thirteen years old. His keen mind readily absorbed the required studies in languages, logic, arithmetic, natural science, and some astronomy. By his senior year the "new philosophy" of Descartes, Boyle, Locke, and Newton were in vogue. He most likely read Locke in his senior year or by his first year of graduate studies. He had established the habit, as instructed by his father, of always keeping a writing pad with him to take down notes. His "Notes on the Mind" reflect reading Locke and interact directly with Lockean ideas.

The reading of Locke was an important intellectual moment for the young Edwards. He writes that he read Locke with more pleasure "than the most greedy miser finds, when gathering up handfuls of silver and gold, from some newly discovered treasure."[7] Modern Edwardsean scholarship has rejected the earlier contention of Perry Miller that Edwards followed Lockean psychology to the degree that he became "America's greatest sensationalist."[8] However, most scholars agree that Edwards draws heavily from Locke's "simple idea" to develop a complex understanding of epistemology. I will turn to this in more detail later. For the moment it is important to note that Edwards embraced Locke's epistemological starting point. Sang Lee points out that "Edwards accepted the fundamental concerns of Locke's empiricism. Knowledge is to be attained through a direct contact with the world. But then, how can the mind also be active in the knowledge process? Edwards did not soften the issue but faced it head-on."[9]

Edwards was also steeped in the theology of Calvinism. In his treatise on the freedom of the will he says that he is willing "to be called a Calvinist, for distinction's sake: though I utterly disclaim a dependence on Calvin, or believing the doctrines which I hold, because he believed and taught them; and cannot be justly charged with believing in every thing just as he taught."[10] It is important to understand Edwards in the

---

7. Murray, *Jonathan Edwards*, 64.
8. Miller, "Edwards, Locke," 134.
9. Lee, *Philosophical Theology*, 124.
10. Edwards, "Freedom of Will," 3.

framework of Puritan Calvinist tradition. This is not to downplay the originality of Edwards's thought, but rather, to locate it within a broad classification of theological tradition.

Edwards would wrestle with the integration of his Puritan Calvinist theology and the lessons of modern thought. Locke and Newton would be read alongside hundreds of theological works cited in the catalogue of reading that Edwards kept through his years at Yale. His wrestling would often take the form of "miscellanies" that he recorded in notebooks as the insights came to him. Throughout his later years one can see the reflections of these early insights in his work as a student and later as a tutor at Yale.

Conversion Experience

In his *Personal Narrative* Edwards articulates his own experience of conversion when he was seventeen years old. This account of the affected heart is a significant part of understanding Edwards and his subsequent theology. One might say that the rest of his life was devoted to understanding this experience and explaining its importance for the advancement of the Christian faith. Three components of the *Narrative* are of particular interest.

THE SENSORY EXPERIENCE OF CONVERSION

It was upon reading 1 Tim 1:17, "Now unto the King eternal, immortal, invisible, the only wise God, be honor and glory for ever and ever, Amen," that Edwards encountered God in a way that profoundly affected him. He wrote,

> As I read the words, there came into my soul, and was as it were diffused through it, a sense of the glory of the Divine Being; a new sense quite different from any thing I ever experienced before. Never any words of scripture seemed to me as these words did. I thought with myself, how excellent a Being that was, and how happy I should be, if I might enjoy that God, and be rapt up in him in heaven, and be as it were swallowed up in him for ever![11]

His experience of God's glory being "diffused" through his soul was "different from anything" he had experienced before. God's presence and

---

11. Edwards, "Memoirs," xiii.

majesty thoroughly moved through him. He often referred to his conversion experience as a "new sense," as above where he wrote of "a sense of the glory of the Divine Being" and "a new sense quite different." This sensory notion of the experience of the soul is an important feature in Edwards's theological system. He continued, "An *inward, sweet sense* of these things, at times, came into my heart; and my soul was led away in pleasant views and contemplations of them."[12] And again, "The *sense I had of divine things*, would often of a sudden kindle up, as it were, a sweet burning in my heart, an ardour of soul, that I know not how to express."[13]

The experiential component of his conversion should not be underplayed. He experienced the presence of God as "a sweet burning in my heart" and found it impossible to express the experience of this soul's "ardour" in words. His personal narrative expresses an experience of knowing God that became a passionate pursuit in his theological system throughout his life. At the core of Edwardsean theology is an experiential understanding of the divine/human encounter that draws deeply from his own experience of conversion.

Edwards continues in his *Narrative* to express the thought that his "former" experiences of God "never reached the heart." As he says, "The delights which I now felt in the things of religion, were of an exceedingly different kind from those before mentioned, that I had when a boy; and what then I had no more notion of, than one born blind has of pleasant and beautiful colours."[14]

The idea of the heart "sensing" God's active presence became an important component of Edwards's theology, though he admits in his *Narrative* that this did not first occur to him: "But it never came into my thought, that there was anything spiritual, or of a saving nature, in this (new sort of affection)."[15] His biographer, Iain Murray, points out that this idea of conversion as a "new sense" or "affection" of the heart did not fit the schemata that were laid out at that time by ministers in New England as the "pattern" for conversion. While he read with interest his grandfather's books on "saving conversion," his diary from 1722 to 1723 indicates concern over his own salvation in that he had not experienced

---

12. Ibid. (emphasis added).
13. Ibid. (emphasis added).
14. Ibid.
15. Ibid.

God's saving grace in the "steps" that Stoddard and other spiritual leaders set forth:

> Dec. 18 [1722] The reason why I in the least question my interest in God's love and favour is: 1. Because I cannot speak so fully to my experience of that preparatory work of which divines speak; 2. I do not remember that I experienced regeneration exactly in those steps in which divines say it is generally wrought ...[16]

Thus he regarded his own experience of beholding God's beauty with some suspicion. It did not fit the required pattern for conversion within the parameters argued for by the religious leadership of the day. However, he would continue to explore the meaning of his own religious experience and develop a theological system in which this experience might be best understood as related to the repetition of the character of God in time and space. As he advanced in theological ingenuity, his ability to integrate this experience with the traditional framework of Puritan Calvinism resulted in some of his most original theological exposition.

Beauty and Its Correlation with the Person of God

Through his conversion Edwards experienced a connection between nature and the presence of God in such a way that he would, ever after, seek to find ways of expressing the relationship of God to the world. In his *Narrative* he tells of one such experience:

> Not long after I first began to experience these things, I gave an account to my father of some things that had passed in my mind. I was pretty much affected by the discourse we had together; and when the discourse was ended, I walked abroad alone, in a solitary place in my father's pasture for contemplation. And as I was walking there, and looking upon the sky and clouds, there came into my mind so sweet a sense of the glorious majesty and grace of God, as I know not how to express—I seemed to see them both in sweet conjunction; majesty and meekness joined together: it was a sweet, and gentle, and holy majesty; and also a majestic meekness.[17]

This vision of the sky and clouds as the "majestic meekness" of God was a new apprehension of things for him. He continues:

---

16. Edwards, "Memoirs," xxiv (emphasis added).
17. Ibid., xiii.

> The appearance of every thing was altered; there seemed to be, as it were, a calm, sweet cast or appearance of divine glory, in almost every thing. God's excellency, his wisdom, his purity, and love, seemed to appear in every thing; in the sun, the moon, and stars; in the clouds and blue sky; in the grass, flowers, trees; in the water and all nature.[18]

He would later incorporate this new apprehension of things into his theological discourses, trying to understand the correlation between nature and God's presence. How did God express his being in the world? What is the connection between our actions and God's actions? These thoughts preoccupied Edwards for years to come. Toward the end of his life he was able to articulate some of his conclusions. Prior to the dissertation on *The Nature of True Virtue*, he wrote a dissertation entitled *Concerning the End for Which God Created the World*. These two works must be read together in order to understand his views on virtue.[19]

For the moment, however, it is important to recognize that in Edwards's own experience of conversion, there was a connection between the attributes of God and the beauty of nature. Beauty, in fact, was to become one of the unifying themes in his theology. He would even go as far as to say that God is beauty. He would not say that beauty is God, however. Beauty was the expression of the divine nature infinitely repeated in time and space.

When it comes to his moral vision or conception of the moral life, Edwards would connect beauty with goodness. Roland Delattre, one of the important interpreters of Edwards's aesthetic vision, offers three guiding propositions with regard to this connection. First, *beauty is the measure of goodness*. "It is itself the highest good and is the distinguishing mark that designates whatever is highest in goodness, especially moral goodness."[20] Second, *beauty designates what is most objective in goodness*. In Edwards's thought, says Delattre, there is "a virtual identification of beauty and excellence."[21] The foundation of goodness is beauty. This identification of excellence and beauty is an important interpre-

---

18. Ibid.

19. As Paul Ramsey notes, "Interpretations of *True Virtue* made without regard to its connection with *End of Creation* have fostered inadequate and even quite mistaken understandings of his ethical writings" (Ramsey, *Ethical Writings*, 6).

20. Delattre, *Beauty and Sensibility*, 71.

21. Ibid.

tive clue to his aesthetic theology. He would delineate these distinctions more carefully in the two dissertations. Delattre's third proposition is that *beauty designates what is most attractive in goodness*. Here Delattre explains an important distinction in Edwards's aesthetic theology—that between "primary" and "secondary" beauty.

> Spiritual or primary beauty may then be said to be the law governing the moral world, just as the secondary and derivative beauty of proportion and harmony may be said to be the law governing the natural world. Beauty is the model of order for both moral and natural worlds, and the relation between the two kinds of beauty (consent and proportion) is the assurance that the two orders are ultimately one under the sovereign pleasure of God.[22]

As Delattre's comments indicate, the idea of beauty was integrative for Edwards. The moral life is connected to nature through the unity of primary and secondary beauty in the expressed sovereignty of God.

Impressions on the Mind

Edwards's conversion narrative contains a third significant component: the "impressions" that came to his mind.

> From about that time I began to have a new kind of apprehensions and ideas about Christ, and the work of redemption, and the glorious way of salvation by him . . . This I know not how to express otherwise, than by a calm, sweet abstraction of soul from all the concerns of the world; and sometimes a kind of vision, or fixed ideas and imaginations, of being alone in the mountains, or some solitary wilderness, far from all mankind, sweetly conversing with Christ, and wrapt and swallowed up in God.[23]

Edwards does not say "new apprehensions and ideas" but rather "*a new kind* of apprehensions and ideas." He recognizes that something is new in this religious experience for him. He is apprehending in a different way, as though his "soul" is "abstracted" from "all the concerns of the world." He would spend much time in his writings defining the nature of authentic religious encounters. No doubt his own experience of having this new kind of apprehension was an important factor in his search for the characteristics of authentic religious experience.

---

22. Ibid.
23. Edwards, "Memoirs," xiii.

His study of Locke's empiricism would give him the language he needed to express these nuances; although, as has already been noted, he cannot be seen as a Lockean empiricist. It was the impressions on the mind that he himself experienced in his conversion that would become the basis for his epistemology of religious experience.

Early Pastoral Experience

Edwards's first experience of pastoral ministry followed the completion of his college degree at Yale. He was licensed for the ministry in 1722 at age eighteen, and "when a request came to New England from Presbyterians in New York for a supply preacher for a new congregation, it was Edwards's name that was recommended."[24] Little is known about his time spent in New York but biographers emphasize this as a period when he consolidated his own spiritual life. It was during this period that he wrote his "Resolutions."[25] The resolutions reflect something of his earnest desire to be serious in his religious devotion. It is important to reflect briefly on the nature of these resolutions because they have a bearing on his conception of the moral life. Over the period of nine months in New York he wrote seventy resolutions, which can be classified into four categories. Below are representative excerpts:

(i) Spiritual fervency

1. Resolved, that I will do whatsoever I think to be most to the glory of God, and my own good, profit, and pleasure, in the whole of my duration; without any consideration of the time, whether now, or never so many myriads of ages hence. Resolved, to do whatever I think to be my duty, and most for the good advantage of mankind in general. Resolved, so to do, whatever difficulties I meet with, how many soever, and how great soever.

4. Resolved, Never to do any manner of thing, whether in soul or body, less or more, but what tends to the glory of God, nor be, nor suffer it, if I can possibly avoid it.

26. Resolved, To cast away such things as I find do abate my assurance.

---

24. Murray, *Jonathan Edwards*, 41.

25. The "Resolutions" were written between December 18, 1722 and August 17, 1723. All of the resolutions are reprinted in Edwards, "Memoirs," xx–xxii.

28. Resolved, To study the Scriptures so steadily, constantly, and frequently, as that I may find, and plainly perceive, myself to grow in the knowledge of the same.

30. Resolved, To strive every week to be brought higher in religion, and to a higher exercise of grace, than I was the week before.

44. Resolved, That no other end but religion shall have any influence at all on any of my actions; and that no action shall be, in the least circumstance, any otherwise than the religious end will carry it.

(ii) Intellectual commitments

11. Resolved, When I think of any theorem in divinity to be solved, immediately to do what I can towards solving it, if circumstances do not hinder it.

(iii) Personal relationships

13. Resolved, To be endeavouring to find out fit objects of liberality and charity.

14. Resolved. Never to do anything out of revenge.

31. Resolved, Never to say anything at all against anybody, but when it is perfectly agreeable to the highest of christian honour, and of love to mankind, agreeable to the lowest humility, and sense of my own faults and failings, and agreeable to the golden rule; often, when I have said anything against any one, to bring it to, and try it strictly by, the test of this Resolution.

47. Resolved, To endeavour, to my utmost, to deny whatever is not most agreeable to a good and universally sweet and benevolent, quiet, peaceable, contented and easy, compassionate and generous, humble and meek, submissive and obliging, diligent and industrious, charitable and even, patient, moderate, forgiving, and sincere, temper; and to do, at all times, what such a temper would lead me to; and to examine strictly, at the end of every week, whether I have done so.

66. Resolved, That I will endeavour always to keep a benign aspect, and air of acting and speaking, in all places, and in all companies, except it should so happen that duty requires otherwise.

70. Let there be something of benevolence in all that I speak.

(iv) Self discipline

5. Resolved, Never to lose one moment of time, but to improve it in the most profitable way I possibly can.

17. Resolved, That I will live so, as I shall wish I had done when I come to die.

20. Resolved, To maintain the strictest temperance in eating and drinking.

37. Resolved, To inquire every night, as I am going to bed, wherein I have been negligent,—what sin I have committed,—and wherein I have denied myself; also, at the end of every week, month, and year.

41. Resolved, To ask myself, at the end of every day, week, month, and year, wherein I could possibly, in any respect, have done better.

56. Resolved, Never to give over, nor in the least to slacken, my fight with corruptions, however unsuccessful I may be.

67. Resolved, After afflictions, to inquire, what I am the better for them; what good I have got by them; and, what I might have got by them.

The seriousness with which Edwards took his spirituality and his ministerial vocation is evident in these resolutions. It is not surprising to see this zeal and enthusiasm for serious religion, given his background in the parsonage. However, what implications are there for the development of his pastoral theology from these resolutions? How might these personal commitments have worked themselves out in future pastoral activities?

Ultimately, Edwards was unsuccessful in integrating his own theological construct of virtue with his approach to pastoral ministry. In the "Resolutions" are seeds of what would become a rigid moral pastoral code in his subsequent ministry. Ideas of virtue expressed toward the end of his life reflect a broader vision than he was able to integrate into his own ministerial activities, as examined below. Why is it that, precisely at the point where his theological vision provided a model for ministry that would go beyond stilted moralism, he embraced the pastoral strictness of his day?

Five months after presenting himself as a candidate, Edwards signed his name in the Northampton Town Book on February 15, 1727. At twenty-three years of age he was hardly able to conceive of the responsibilities that were awaiting him upon the death of his grandfather only two years later. In his early years at Northampton he was well liked by all. While the aging Stoddard had been unable to give pastoral attention to the teaching of youth and children, Edwards seemed to relish these responsibilities. He organized the young people into classes and would meet with them regularly, instructing them in the faith.

With his grandfather's death in 1729, Edwards was given the opportunity to establish himself as the worthy successor. His ability in the pulpit was above average, though health concerns occasionally set him back. That his ministry was well received is indicated by the fact that, during a period of illness that required him to be absent from the pulpit, he returned from New Haven to find that in the months he was away "a good large barn" had been built for him.

One of the factors affecting congregational life in this period was the common assertion by clergy that the church was in a period of decline. Throughout the early 1700s, preaching in New England emphasized the moral failings of the people and lamented the "decline of religion." One of his biographers captures the spirit of the clergy well:

> From the pulpit, religion was preached not as an inner satisfaction of the spirit but as a code of abstinence from such defilements as husking bees, journeys, and unsuitable discourse on the Sabbath, bonfires and fireworks on Lecture Thursday. Unaware of their inconsistency, preachers inveighed heavily against the doctrine of "Good Works" and then proceeded to make a formula for American godliness in terms of the 1620's.[26]

The Puritan context of pastoral work, then, served to undermine the passionate Edwards. His experience of conversion, though important to the formation of his spirituality, gave way to the broader concerns of protecting the church against the perils of Arminianism and the "avalanche of debauchery" displayed by swearing, Sabbath-breaking, and smoking in the streets. Soon these concerns became the functional norm for the developing pastor. A second ministerial function was to preoccupy Edwards in the coming years. On July 8, 1731, he distinguished himself as a spokesperson for Calvinism in a lecture delivered at Harvard University, "God Glorified in Man's Dependence." This inaugural lecture became his first published work[27] and broadened his ministry to include the defense of the traditional Puritan Calvinism.

---

26. Winslow, *Jonathan Edwards*, 100.

27. "God Glorified in Man's Dependence," was published in August, 1731. See the reprint listed in the bibliography.

But he was uncomfortable with the personal responsibilities of the ministry. He often withdrew from his people into the privacy of his study, and was not in the habit of visiting his congregation as some ministers were prone to do. In October of 1731 the Association of ministers went on record to declare their conviction that "the catechizing of children . . . belonged in the home and should be kept there."[28] This suited Edwards well and was to be his pastoral style throughout his years at Northampton. He continued the practice of meeting with small groups of children and young people and prepared questions for young converts. However, his involvement with the lives of people in his parish was at arm's length, following the custom of a more aristocratic clergy of the eighteenth century.

The predominant focus of his work was preaching. Week after week he would rise in the pulpit to declare the whole counsel of God. His style was not particularly buoyant, though in later years he would engage in more passionate discourse. He wrote out his sermons in manuscript, unlike his grandfather who considered this practice to be among the signs of an ineffective ministry. He carefully articulated his sermons in a predictable pattern of text, outline of main points, doctrinal clarification, and application. Often the sermons were more like treatises, such as his discourse on "Justification by Faith Alone,"[29] which commands thirty-two finely printed pages including detailed footnotes. About his preaching style one of his biographers writes:

> The making of sermons was to Jonathan Edwards one of the chief ends of his reading, his study and his thought . . . in relation to his flock he was more of a preacher than a pastor. . . . It was on Sunday morning at the ringing of the meetinghouse bell that Northampton had its best chance to know "Mr. Edwards," as he mounted his high pulpit and in a quiet voice, without movement or gesture, laid down his doctrine. His tall, spare figure and his deliberate manner gave him a commanding presence. . . . Every word was distinctly spoken. . . . This delicate-looking young man had something to say, and strangely enough his fragility seemed to increase his power.[30]

---

28. Winslow, *Jonathan Edwards*, 120.
29. Included in Dwight, ed., *Works of Edwards*, 1:622–54.
30. Winslow, *Jonathan Edwards*, 129.

Edwards took his mandate seriously. He desired to see those entrusted to his charge converted and growing in their faith.

In 1733 he noticed some changes particularly among the "young people." He noticed a certain "unusual flexibleness" and "yielding to advice" on their part after a sermon on the evil tendency of "making mirth" on the evening of the Sabbath. Evidently the young people themselves took this message to heart and "were willing of themselves to comply with the counsel."

This new found "flexibleness" was reinforced in its seriousness by the sudden death of two persons in the area. In April of 1734, in a village about three miles from town, "there happened a very *sudden and awful death of a young man in the bloom of his youth*; who being violently seized with a *pleurisy*, and taken immediately very *delirious*, died in about *two days*."[31] It seems that the young people were quite struck by the timing of this death and their own new-found obedience, which reinforced their tendency towards continued flexibility.

The same is true of the second case, a married woman who, although gravely ill, was concerned about her spiritual well-being. Edwards observes that she had experienced "satisfying evidences of God's saving mercy," so that she died "very full of comfort."[32]

Again the young people seemed startled and affected. Edwards does not say that the young people were motivated to continue their spiritual renewal because of fear, but he closely associates the renewed interest in religion among the young people with these events. As the pastor, he "proposed to the young people" that they meet for "social religion" and divide themselves into several small groups to meet in various parts of the town. These groups did in fact meet and Edwards was pleased at the spiritual progress of his young people.

In 1734 and 1735 the Northampton parish was to experience the first "awakening." By the end of this period over three hundred persons had professed their conversion. Several noticeable changes happened in his ministry during this period. In his desire to see the genuine revival of religion in his congregation Edwards moved towards a more denunciatory style of preaching. Ola Winslow records the following:

---

31. Edwards, "Faithful Narrative," 347 (author's emphasis).
32. Ibid.

Relentlessly he called the roll of the town sins which shut men out from God's mercy and kindled the divine wrath to their destruction. "How many kinds of wickedness are there?" he asked, and then proceeded to answer his own question: irreverence in God's house, disregard of the Sabbath, neglect of family prayer, disobedience to parents, quarrelling, greediness, sensuality, hatred of one's neighbor. The list was no other than a roll call of the Seven Deadlies in village dress.[33]

The revival itself was initiated by the conversion of a town woman who was notably one of the greatest "company keepers" in the whole town. This surprising conversion was the first of many and the sure evidence that something genuine from God was taking place in Northampton. At first Edwards was concerned that this person might bring ill repute to the revival of religion, but to his delight, "many went to talk with her, concerning what she had met with; and what appeared in her seemed to be to the satisfaction of all that did so."[34]

In 1736 he gave testimony of surprising changes in the community:

> When once the Spirit of God began to be so wonderfully poured out in a general way through the town, people had soon done with their old quarrels, backbitings, and intermeddling with other men's matters. The tavern was soon left empty, and persons kept very much at home; none went abroad unless on necessary business, or on some religious account, and every day seemed like a Sabbath-day.[35]

Edwards recognized the changes that were happening in the spiritual life of Northampton. He seems to have adjusted his pastoral work to organize the young people and to do what he could to sustain the revival of religion in his community.

In his *Faithful Narrative* he observes further that the "awakening" was taking place in all age sectors of the community. It was happening among the older generation:

> It has been heretofore rarely heard of, that any were converted past middle age; but now we have the same ground to think, that many such have at this time been savingly changed, as that others

33. Winslow, *Jonathan Edwards*, 153.
34. Edwards, "Faithful Narrative," 348.
35. Ibid., 351.

> have been so in more early years. I suppose there were upwards of fifty persons converted in this town above forty years of age; more than twenty of them above fifty; about ten of them above sixty; and two of them above seventy years of age.[36]

And it was happening among the children as well:

> It has heretofore been looked on as a strange thing, when any have seemed to be savingly wrought upon and remarkably changed in their childhood. But now, I suppose, near thirty were, to appearance, savingly wrought upon, between ten and fourteen years of age; two between nine and ten, and one of about four years of age.[37]

Edwards goes on to describe some of the unique characteristics of those who were being converted, giving special attention to two particular cases. There was the case of Abigail Hutchinson, who struggled for her spiritual well-being despite the inflammation of her throat that prevented her from eating anything and who "died chiefly of famine." There was also the case of the four-year-old, Phebe Bartlet. Both of these cases seem to point to extreme emotional upheaval. What is it that he was trying to affirm in his account of the revival at Northampton?

I believe that he was concerned to make a case for the vitality of the changes that were being wrought in the people of Northampton from young to old. "Company-keeping" women were being "savingly converted"; young people reinforced their seriousness in religion because of mysterious deaths; the dying sought only consolation in Christ, and young children discovered mature ideas of saving faith. In the end, however, it seems that he defeated his own purpose by pointing out these extreme examples.

Is it possible, in other words, that he missed the true pastoral dimension of these important changes by insisting on the continual evidences of conversion? Rather than consoling the dying woman, bringing spiritual comfort to the frightened young child, and alleviating the irrational fears of the young people, Edwards allowed these sufferings and struggles to continue in the hope that they would serve his purposes of continuing the revival. He was no doubt sincere in his desire to see more

---

36. Ibid., 350.
37. Ibid.

people affected by the "awakening," but one wonders if his preoccupation with the events interfered with his pastoral sensibilities.

In any case, the revival soon ended. Edwards noted that about May of 1735 "the Spirit of God was gradually withdrawing,"[38] attributing the change in the community in part to an attempted suicide, and the successful suicide of his uncle, Joseph Hawley, who put "an end to his own life by cutting his throat."[39] Following this there were many in the community who became melancholic about their own life and reported that they, "had it urged upon them as if somebody had spoke to them, 'Cut your own throat, now is a good opportunity. Now! now!'"[40]

Furthermore, the "Springfield controversy"[41] and the congregation's preoccupation with building a new meetinghouse to accommodate all of the new converts added to the shifting tide in Northampton. Though for the most part Edwards up to this point had enjoyed the respect of his parish and established himself as a worthy minister, things were beginning to change and, over the next decade, Edwards would often find himself in controversy with his church.

The "Great Awakening" of 1740 to 1742 pervaded all of New England. The fiery George Whitfield came to America from England and before leaving ignited a flame that few would have thought possible. Though difficult to assess, the number of conversions has been estimated at between thirty and forty thousand persons. Across New England there were great increases in church membership:

> In the parish of Suffield, also in Hampshire County, where the pastor died in April 1741, Edwards appears to have given regu-

---

38. Ibid., 363.
39. Ibid.
40. Ibid.
41. This is the case of Robert Breck. The Hampshire Association, doubting his orthodoxy, had opposed his ordination. The Springfield congregation, resenting their involvement, called a council of Boston ministers to hear the charges and, if they could be overthrown, would proceed with the ordination. On October 7, 1735, when the council convened, Robert Breck stood to defend himself and was arrested by civil authorities and put in prison. This indignity led to the Massachusetts General Assembly vote of censure against the Hampshire Association for their interference in parish concerns. Unfortunately for Edwards, he was the one chosen by the Hampshire Association to draw up their defence, even though he had not been present at the October council. His association with the affair was never forgotten, and, years later when Edwards was confronted with trouble in his parish, it was Robert Breck who would cast the deciding vote against him.

lar help and to have admitted ninety-five new members in the following months. At Hartford twenty-seven were added to the church in 1741; at North Stonington one hundred and four; sixty in six months at the Old South Church in Boston and one hundred and two in twelve months at the New North Church in the same town. Hingham had forty-five admissions in 1741–1742, Plymouth eighty-four and Middleborough one hundred and seventy-four.[42]

Throughout this period Edwards participated in the new practice of itinerant preaching. Whereas prior to the Great Awakening the custom was for the pastor of a parish to preach in his own church, the coming of George Whitfield changed this. It was in Enfield, not his own congregation at Northampton, that Edwards delivered his sermon, *Sinners in the Hands of an Angry God*.[43] He participated in the activities associated with the revival and became one of the most articulate spokespersons in the ensuing debates against the excesses of the "Enthusiasts."

In his own congregation an estimated two hundred persons were converted during this period, though this often happened in his absence. The general increase in religious participation in Edwards's parish was significant, though in many ways, he was losing his influence. He began to lose favor with the congregation throughout this decade, ending in his dismissal from the church in 1750. There were three critical incidents in his ministry through this period leading up to his expulsion: (i) the salary dispute in 1742; (ii) the "bad book" incident of 1744; and (iii) the communion controversy of 1748–1749.

Problems in Ministry

The Salary Dispute

The private affairs of the parsonage were widely discussed in Northampton during the 1740s. Although Northampton had been known to offer a fair salary or, in the language of the Town Record, a "Support suitable & well adapted to that honourable office," the salary was inadequate for the needs of Edwards's growing family. In 1741 he took his case before

---

42. Murray, *Jonathan Edwards*, 166, 167.

43. Preached at Enfield, July 8, 1741. The sermon text was Deut 32:35, "Vengeance is mine, and retribution, in due time their foot will slip; for the day of their calamity is near, and the impending things are hastening upon them." Included in Dwight, ed., *Works of Edwards*, 2:7–12.

the town and was promptly granted an increase along with a renewed commitment for the parish to supply him with wood.

The following spring, an increase of fifty pounds, which he did not personally request, resulted in a "great uneasiness in the town" over pastoral expenditures:

> The standard of living on King Street [Edwards's residence] was sharply criticized, even the clothes the family wore becoming a subject for reproof. Mr. Edwards was of "a craving disposition," abusing the generosity of the town by "lavish" expenditure. So much was said that he was obliged to make public the family budget, in itemized array, and then to suffer still greater humiliation as the parish critics fell upon the list and made it prove their own thesis—just as many children could be maintained for half the sum.[44]

His grandfather, Solomon Stoddard, had become a wealthy man without complaint from the congregation. Now, fifteen years into his ministry at Northampton, Edwards was experiencing underlying resistance and criticism. Though the salary issue was finally settled in 1748 with the offer of a fixed salary, this on-going dispute weighed heavily on Edwards and served to undermine his authority in the parish.

The "Bad Book" Incident

In March of 1744, five or six boys obtained a book of instructions to midwives. Evidently this aroused the curiosity of some young people and the book was passed around. When the incident came to Edwards's attention he immediately launched an investigation into the matter—an appropriate course of action for the minister. At the close of the preaching service, he informed the congregation of what had happened, took a vote authorizing the investigation of the incident, and appointed a time for the committee to meet. All of these proceedings were according to the custom of the time. What proved to be a critical error, however, was that he proceeded to list the names of young people who were to appear at the investigation without separating the innocent from the culprits, thus seeming to inculpate individuals who were preparing, rather, to testify against the accused. This action outraged the people of Northampton parish and for the next two months there were very uneasy relations between pulpit and parish.

44. Winslow, *Jonathan Edwards*, 201.

The matter was drawn to a close on June 3rd but not before twenty-two witnesses were prevailed upon in the rigorous investigation. The nature of the contents of the book, its various hiding places, the names of those who read it and/or listened to the discussions of it were all matters of concern. In the end, the public confession of three of the ringleaders, Timothy and Simeon Root, and Oliver Warner, were read by the pastor and the matter was completed.

The mishandling of this affair was not something that Edwards could afford in the rocky days of his ministry at Northampton. He seems to have felt throughout the affair that his pastoral authority was at stake. The establishment of a committee to assist in internal matters in 1740 was an indication that the previous era of pastoral prerogatives was under challenge. The combination of the mishandling of the affair, his waning popularity in the parish, and the general challenges to his ecclesial authority made the next number of years increasingly difficult for Edwards.

Undaunted by the incident, Edwards continued to admonish his congregation, viewing this as his solemn responsibility as a minister of the gospel. To the young people, who years before had heeded his counsel by their own volition, he preached a sermon in the fall of 1744 using Ps 144:12, "That our sons may be as plants grown up in their youth; that our daughters may be as corner stones, polished after the similitude of a palace." Introducing this theme he stated:

> 'Tis a peculiarly lovely and pleasant sight to behold young People walking in that ways of vertue and piety ... I dare appeal to those young People that have in a great measure neglected Relig.[ion] & given the Reins to their inclination & spent a great Deal of their time over wine mirth & those Diversions that are inconsistent with a serious religion.[45]

This time there was no response from the young people and no great desire to heed the warning of the pastor in these matters of virtue and piety. As a result, the young people were pressured to conform to the will of the church leaders. In the public record of the Town Book the following year, legislation was enacted for the prosecuting "of the Irreverent

---

45. Ibid., 211–12.

and disorderly behavior of many of the young people and children in the house of God in the time of publick worship."[46]

THE COMMUNION CONTROVERSY

When Edwards challenged the policy of admitting all to the Lord's Supper, a practice long established under Solomon Stoddard, he sealed his fate at the Northampton parish. In 1748, a new communicant sought membership at the Northampton parish. Edwards used this occasion to take a stand on an issue that he had been silent about for twenty-two years. He had been convinced for some time that church members must be able to profess sincere belief in their own "renovation of heart" before participating in the Lord's Supper. Four different wordings of a proposed declaration were submitted to a committee for approval. All four were rejected.

Edwards sought to defend his new position and asked the congregation to allow him to publish a treatise on the matter, to which they agreed. In the *Preface* he writes about the gravity of the issue:

> I can truly say, on account of this and some other considerations, it is what I engage in with the greatest reluctance that ever I undertook any public service in my life... I am conscious, not only is the interest of religion concerned in this affair, but my own reputation, future usefulness, and my very subsistence, all seem to depend on my freely opening and defending myself, as to my principles, and agreeable conduct in my pastoral charge.[47]

Though the work contained a broad defense from Scripture for his position, the congregation was not persuaded. A council was established to determine whether he should be dismissed since he and the congregation had different views on the matter. On June 22, 1750, after three days of deliberation, the council voted to dismiss him from his pulpit. The congregational vote was 23 for and 230 against supporting the pastor. His fate was sealed.

On July 2, 1750, he preached his farewell sermon. The title page indicates that it was delivered "after the people's public rejection of their minister, and renouncing their relations to him as pastor of the church

---

46. Ibid., 212. Action of Dec. 20, 1745, as noted by Winslow from the papers of the Andover Collection.
47. Edwards, "Preface to An Humble Inquiry," 434.

there... occasioned by difference of sentiments, concerning the requisite qualifications of members of the church in complete standing."[48]

The language of "public rejection of their minister" indicates the pain with which Edwards descended the pulpit at Northampton. In his sermon he bids friends and enemies alike to keep in mind the "solemn meeting on the day of the Lord." He confesses:

> I have found the work of the ministry among you to be a great work indeed, a work of exceeding care, labour, and difficulty. Many have been the heavy burdens that I have borne in it, to which my strength has been very unequal... But now I have reason to think my work is finished which I had to do as your minister: you have publicly rejected me, and my opportunities cease.[49]

After the many blessings of the revival of 1734–1735 and the Great Awakening of 1740–1742, this final defeat and rejection was extremely difficult for him.

After a brief stint as supply pastor at Northampton, Edwards accepted the post of missionary to the Indians at Stockbridge, Massachusetts. During his time there (1751–1757) he was able to devote himself to his work with the Indians and to writing some of his most important works: *Freedom of the Will, Original Sin, Concerning the End for Which God Created the World* and *The Nature of True Virtue*.[50] Released from the difficulties associated with the pastorate in Northampton, he was able to articulate a vision for the moral life that is quite different from the one reflected in his ministry there.

In 1758 he was chosen to be the new President of New Jersey College (Princeton). He arrived on February 16, 1758, but died only one month later (March 22, 1758) from complications from a smallpox inoculation. His burial in the Princeton cemetery symbolized his estrangement from Northampton parish.

---

48. Edwards, "Farewell Sermon," cxcviii.

49. Ibid., cciv.

50. These two works, *Concerning the End for Which God Created the World*, and *The Nature of True Virtue* were published as Part I and II under the title *Two Dissertations*. They were written in Stockbridge in 1755 and published posthumously in 1765.

ISSUES IN THE DEVELOPMENT OF EDWARDS'S MORAL VISION

In the section to follow I wish to show *how* and perhaps *why* Edwards failed to integrate his theological ideas of virtue with his pastoral practice. My purpose is to isolate some of the key issues related to the development of a pastoral theology of virtue. Here I will argue that, as a pastor, Edwards faced some of the same fundamental dilemmas that all pastors face in integrating their theological ethic with their pastoral work. In doing this I hope, further, to be able to isolate some important clues in the formation of Edwards's idea of virtue that will be discussed later in the development of a construct of virtue for pastoral theology.

The Culture Trap

Puritan New England was an exacting society. Few understood this as well as Jonathan Edwards who "toed the line" while a tutor at Yale, as the young successor to one of the most important pulpits of the day, and as one of the chief defenders of Puritan doctrine against the excesses of the Enthusiasts and the errors of the Arminians.

Edwards inherited a world of responsibility that he defines in his farewell sermon at Northampton as "a work of exceeding care, labour, and difficulty" with a multitude of "heavy burdens." In light of the fact that he conceived himself as the defender of Puritan doctrines, one might begin to see the risks associated with his writing and publications. If they did not match the practices of his predecessors, he would undermine the very religious culture that he loved and understood as his particular place in the world. With regard to the moral life in general we see his pastoral practice upholding the tradition. He is vigilant against the evils of Sabbath-breaking, "wine mirth," and other social "mischief." In a sense he is functioning very much as a minister in Puritan New England would be expected to.

How very different this is from the vision of virtue that he articulates in his dissertation of 1755. In that work he almost never mentions these moralistic social problems but is intent on offering a positive vision for the moral life grounded in love for God. His effort throughout the volume is to express virtue as a kind of beauty or "consent to Being." Where he does speak about sin, his effort is to show its roots in "self-love not subordinate to a regard to being in general,"[51] and how habituated pride and sensuality serve to "diminish a sense of conscience."[52] These more mature views of the moral life were not apparent in his ministerial practice through the years, though it is conceivable that he held such views personally.

It is difficult to explain the difference between Edwards's expressed moral vision in *True Virtue* and his pastoral practice without at least considering the possibility that he was functioning largely within a framework expected of him as a Puritan pastor rather than according to the compass of his own moral vision. It may well be that he was not even able to articulate his own theory of virtue until he had long moved away from the context of Northampton and the formal responsibilities of minister in a notable congregation.

To assist in understanding this problem, Peter Berger's discussion of the social construction of reality is helpful. Berger asserts that the function of language in the social construction of reality has an ontological basis, i.e., "the language exists because he [the individual in society], along with others, continues to employ it."[53] Thus, the continuation of the dialogue with culture produces the culture itself so that "it may be said that the individual keeps 'talking back' to the world that formed him and thereby continues to maintain the latter as reality."[54] What if the person stops "talking back" or abruptly withdraws from the conversation with culture? According to Berger, such a person would become "worldless,"[55] for the "world begins to shake in the very instant that its sustaining conversation begins to falter."[56]

In one sense, Edwards was particularly engaged in the language-forming structure of Puritan culture. His articulation of the religious experiences of the revivals of 1735 and 1740 are among the most penetrating expressions found anywhere. They are engaged with the issues of the day, and on these religious experiences Edwards could be considered a "shaper" of Puritan society. He expresses his perspectives on the religious life using the internal language of the church common to his

---

51. Edwards, *True Virtue*, 92.
52. Ibid., 93.
53. Berger, *Sacred Canopy*, 19.
54. Ibid.
55. Ibid., 21.
56. Ibid., 22.

day. In this respect he must be understood as a voice within a particular religious culture.

With regards to his moral vision, however, Edwards became "worldless." Though in pastoral practice he upheld and enforced a rigid moral code that condemned seemingly trivial aspects of religious life, he did not himself hold such a myopic view of the moral life. The incongruence between his private views and his public responsibility may have been one of the factors leading to his eventual parting with the Northampton congregation. This possibility becomes plausible when Berger's discussion of "legitimation" is taken into account. He defines legitimation as "socially objectivated 'knowledge' that serves to explain and justify the social order."[57]

For Berger, there is an objective and a subjective aspect to legitimation, both of which are required for the maintenance of the legitimation itself. He argues that "the reality of the world as socially defined must be maintained externally, in the conversation of men with each other, as well as internally, in the way by which the individual apprehends the world within his own consciousness."[58]

If a person's subjective/internal apprehension of a socially defined construct, such as virtue, did not match up with the world that was being maintained by the "traditional affirmations," "moral maxims," and "myths" of the society at large, the result would be that such a person would become "worldless." Due to the incongruence between the subjective and objective, legitimation would cease to be maintained. This, in my view, is precisely what took place in Edwards's case.

I have chosen to isolate this problem because of its importance for a construction of a pastoral theology of virtue. In a sense the problem is a common one for the pastor. The community of faith expresses a worldview that is maintained through legitimation. As a spokesperson for the community, the pastor is expected to sustain this worldview. This is one of the primary functions expected of the spokesperson.

If the pastor, however, is developing private views that go beyond the pre-theoretical assumptions of the community, he or she is confronted by the choice of either continuing the legitimation (as expected) or becoming "worldless." This is the "culture trap." Moral communities

---

57. Ibid., 29.
58. Ibid., 32.

are particularly prone to this problem because they exist as a kind of "counter-culture."

In my view, Edwards's private perceptions of the moral life were incongruent with the moralistic codes of Puritan church life.[59] Ironically, his positive and constructive vision for the moral life was incompatible with the religiously legitimated views of Puritan New England. This tension between his public responsibility as a minister in New England and the internal development of his moral vision created an untenable future for him.

Images for Ministry

Images profoundly affect the way one approaches ministry. Images become the functional paradigm, as it were, of how ministry is done. I will explore this idea in relationship to Edwards's own approach to pastoral ministry. I have already noted that to understand him correctly on virtue theory one must understand the pastoral framework from which he operated. Like other pastors he had images of ministry that guided his practice. What were these?

In a study of Edwards's published and unpublished ordination sermons, Helen Petter Westra encapsulates some of the images that Edwards uses to express his understanding of the pastoral vocation. She contends that Edwards needs to be understood primarily as a pastor and takes his ordination sermons to be the documents that "most clearly reveal his conception and enactments of that office."[60] Furthermore, she argues that "an exploration of the images or metaphors . . . is helpful in understanding the ways in which Edwards viewed himself as a minister."[61]

She identifies nine particular images that Edwards uses in his ordination sermons: steward, watchman, ambassador, messenger, anointed one, bridegroom, light, trumpet, and savior. Another important image is suggested in a funeral message preached on the occasion of the inter-

---

59. Berger contends that there are five levels on which legitimation functions: (1) self-legitimating facticity; (2) challenges to facticity; (3) pre-theoretical affirmations (tradition, proverbs/moral maxims, myths); (4) theoretical bodies of "knowledge"; (5) highly theoretical constructions. He suggests that very few persons are actually interested in the highly theoretical level of "ideas." I contend that Edwards's theoretical construct of virtue was in conflict with the pre-theoretical notions of Puritan New England. See ibid., 31–32.

60. Westra, "Above All Others," 209.

61. Ibid., 210.

ment of the Rev. Mr. William Williams—the image of "father." In order to isolate the broad themes of his vision for the pastoral vocation I will categorize these images under three broader headings: (1) images of voice; (2) images of action; and (3) images of personhood. I will explore these for their affirmations and conceptions of the pastoral office, the aim being to uncover Edwards's self-perception in his work as the minister at Northampton and to isolate problems involved in the integration of his moral vision with his approach to the pastoral office.

IMAGES OF VOICE: MESSENGER AND TRUMPET

Edwards conceived the ministry primarily in terms of speaking the Word. In his farewell sermon at Northampton, he conveys this image of the pastor as "messenger." "Ministers are his messengers, sent forth by him; and, in their office and administrations among their people, represent his person, stand in his stead, as those that are sent to declare his mind, to do his work, and to speak and act in his name."[62] The messenger is to "declare his [God's] mind" and to "speak ... in his name." In an unpublished ordination sermon ten years earlier, Edwards emphasized the importance of submitting to God's message and superior thoughts:

> Ministers ought not to preach those things which their own wisdom and reason suggest, but the things that are already dictated by the Spirit of God ... Their preaching ought to rely on what [is] revealed and discovered to their minds by an understanding infinitely superior to others.[63]

Edwards does not address the issues of hermeneutics associated with the preaching task. He only conveys the importance of the minister's function as God's messenger. Further, the message is to be conveyed in a way that influences its hearers. Hence the minister's preaching "may be fitly compared to the blowing of a trumpet." The preacher "does what a horn does to speak so as to influence and affect its hearers."[64]

This idea of sensory impression is an important part of his idea of the messenger's work. Perry Miller explains that, for Edwards, "an idea is a unit of experience."[65] He confronted both rationalism and sensa-

62. Edwards, "Farewell Sermon," ccii.

63. Unpublished sermon of May 7, 1740 on 1 Cor 2:11–13, as quoted by Westra, "Above All Others," 211.

64. November, 1733, unpublished sermon on Mic 2:11 as quoted in ibid., 219.

65. Miller, "Edwards, Locke," 131.

tionalism with his epistemology of sensory experience, denying that the appeal to the emotions must always be made at the expense of the idea. Rather, both the emotional and intellectual elements of understanding are required. [Edwards] "was ready to maintain that an emotional response is also an intellectual, or that an intellectual, in the highest sense, is also emotional."[66]

Images of Action: Steward, Watchman, and Light

Something of the activism of the Puritan mindset can be seen in the images of action. The image of a steward is developed in a sermon based on Luke 10:17–18[67] and, as elsewhere in his reflections on this theme, describes the minister as one who has been entrusted with the very work of God. Ministers are "called and set apart to the work [of ministry] with a sufficient signification of Christ's will that when his orders are thus attended, it shall be looked upon as being done in his name."[68]

Edwards maintained this image of ministry as stewardship throughout his life, and in his farewell sermon this theme occurs once again. "Ministers are sent forth by Christ to their people on his business. They are his servants and messengers; and, when they have finished their service, they must return to their master to give him an account of what they have done, and of the entertainment they have had in performing their ministry."[69]

Westra notes an air of exuberance and joy in the 1736 sermon, which she contrasts with the later ordination sermons that treat the "details, circumstances, and especially the difficulties of the minister's work."[70] In 1736 Edwards was occupied with the 300 new converts of his parish and the work of building a new sanctuary. His moods reflect the situation of his parish, though his image of the faithful steward seems to be consistent throughout his ministry.

The image of the "watchman for souls" comes from the title of his sermon preached at the ordination of Jonathan Judd on June 8, 1743. The tone of this sermon reflects the shift in mood observed by Westra.

66. Ibid.

67. An unpublished sermon preached at Lambstown, Massachusetts, November 17, 1736 as cited by Westra, "Above All Others," 210.

68. Cited by ibid.

69. Edwards, "Farewell Sermon," ccii.

70. Westra, "Above All Others," 211.

Edwards portrays a day of accountability for ministers, who will be called at the last judgment to answer to God for their work. To the ministers present at the sermon he urges:

> You are to watch for these souls as one that must give account. If any one of these souls should be missing hereafter, having been lost under your ministry, it will be demanded of you another day, by your great Lord, "What is become of such a soul? Here are not all the souls that I committed to you to bring home to me: there is such an one missing; what is become of it? Has it perished through your neglect?"[71]

In the action images of ministry we can observe an over-developed sense of responsibility. Clearly the responsibility and weighty matters of eternity rest on the shoulders of the entrusted steward. The language of accountability is used persuasively in the ordination sermon of 1743 to heighten the sense of importance attached to the task of ministry so that ministers must carefully weigh "what has become of such a soul." It is notable that, at the time when his own pastoral authority was beginning to be questioned at Northampton, Edwards speaks about the "faithfulness" of the minister as God's "watchman for souls," reinforcing the divine entrustment.

The image of "light" is also used in another ordination sermon of this period with the text John 5:35. Here Edwards insists that the minister is to be "both a burning and a shining light."[72] Westra misses the thrust of the sermon when she conveys the light image of ministry as "animating, illuminating, revealing and warning light for the church and the world."[73] Edwards is rather asserting an important conviction that authentic religious expression is a balance between heat (spiritual warmth and ardor in the heart) and light (human learning, speculative knowledge, and wisdom). Thus the true minister is one who displays both "burning" and "shining" together: "When light and heat are thus united in a minister of the gospel, it shows that each is genuine, and of a right kind, and that both are divine. Divine light is attended with heat;

---

71. From the ordination sermon, "The Great Concern of Watchman for Souls," preached June 8, 1743, in Boston, for the ordination of Jonathan Judd. From Westra, "Above All Others," 219.

72. Edwards, "True Excellency of a Gospel Minister," 958.

73. Westra, "Above All Others", 214.

and so, on the other hand, a truly divine and holy heat and ardour is ever accompanied with light."[74]

As this emphasis on heat with light together is made throughout the sermon, he is asserting not only the illuminating functions of teaching but also the spiritual warmth that comes with genuine ministry. He reiterates throughout the sermon, that "when divine light and heat attend each other in ministers of the gospel, their light will be like the beams of the sun, that do not only convey light, but give life."[75] Thus he maintains that "genuine" ministry is conveyed as a "burning and shining light." He preached this sermon in 1744 in the aftermath of the "Great Awakening," at a time when he was concerned about the excesses of the Enthusiasts and yet unwilling to concede to those who would reduce ministry to rational, disaffected doctrine. The sermon is a preamble to the 1746 work on Religious Affections. The ministerial image that Edwards preferred was not "light" or "heat" but "a burning and shining light."

Images of Personhood: Bridegroom, Anointed One, and Savior

Images that reflect personhood appear in Edwards's later ordination sermons. In a 1746 ordination sermon titled *The Church's Marriage to Her Sons and to Her God*,[76] Edwards uses the imagery of a "proxy bridegroom marrying the church . . . in the name of [the] master."[77] He says, "The uniting of faithful ministers with Christ's people in the ministerial office, when done in due manner, is like a young man's marrying a virgin."[78]

In the use of this image Edwards speaks of the minister as the church's tender lover, a "kind of spiritual husband . . . sent to woo"[79] the beloved. One emphasis he develops in the sermon is the idea that, "because Christ looks on ministers as proxy bridegrooms to his bride, they will be greatly honored in the heavenly celebration of Christ's marriage

---

74. Edwards, "True Excellency of a Gospel Minister," 958.
75. Ibid.
76. Preached at the instalment of the Rev. Mr. Samuel Buell as pastor at East-Hampton on Long Island, September 19, 1746 as cited by Westra, "Above All Others," 219.
77. Cited in ibid., 214.
78. Cited in ibid.
79. Cited in ibid., 214, 215.

to his beloved church."⁸⁰ Viewed in light of the growing unrest in the congregation at Northampton, this image both affirms Edwards's intimate affection and asserts his pastoral authority. The shift from an active image of "steward" or "watchman" to this intimate one of "bridegroom" comes at a time when his personal popularity in his parish was waning.

This shift toward the use of personal images in the later years of his ministry continues with the 1747 imagery of minister as "son of oil" or "anointed one."⁸¹ In this image the minister is seen as a sacred olive branch of Christ, the great Anointed One. The branch is filled with precious oil to convey the riches of God's grace to Christ's church, the golden candlestick, so that it may burn brightly. His purpose in using this image seems to be, once again, to assert pastoral authority as delegated by Christ.

Like the "proxy bridegroom" who loves the church on behalf of Christ, the "son of oil" is the representative of Christ the Anointed One, and appointed by Christ as a means of grace. Thus, he concludes his sermon with a bold appeal to the unity of the minister's authority with the authority of Christ:

> 'Tis the will of Christ to convey that golden oil [of grace], that most precious benefit that ever he bestows, by ministers, whereby as Christ himself is the author of eternal salvation, so ministers become a kind of subordinate savior. Ministers are thus anointed to eternal priesthood and an eternal royalty in heaven and shall be there kings and prophets to . . . the Father.⁸²

The final image that Edwards uses for the minister is that of "savior." He had already used it in the 1747 sermon as "subordinate savior." In his later sermons, particularly after his dismissal from Northampton, the dominant image of the minister is that of the Christlike "savior" who, like the Savior, suffers reproach, rejection, and affliction. In one of his last ordination sermons, on Acts 11:28, Edwards makes his boldest declaration of this image: "The work of the ministry is the same in many respects as Christ's own work, the work of being *savior*."⁸³ As Westra comments on the final ordination sermons: "In contrast to earlier ordination sermons,

---

80. Cited in ibid., 215.

81. Unpublished sermon on Zech 4:12–14 delivered for a ministerial installation in November, 1747, as cited in ibid., 215, 219.

82. Cited in ibid., 216.

83. Cited in ibid., 219 (emphasis added).

these later sermons enlarged upon the pain ... of gospel ministry, identifying strongly with the self-sacrificing, suffering work of Christ."[84]

Edwards became almost completely absorbed in the image of the suffering "savior" in these final sermons. Just as Christ suffered difficulties, sorrow, and reproach:

> Ministers should be persons of the same quiet, lamb-like spirit that Christ was of, the same spirit of submission to God's will, and patience under afflictions, and meekness toward men; of the same calmness and composure of spirit under reproaches and sufferings from the malignity of evil men; of the same spirit of forgiveness of injuries.[85]

CONCLUSION

Throughout this chapter we have explored Edwards's life and ministry in search of clues for interpreting the moral vision expounded in *The Nature of True Virtue*. I have emphasized his life-long calling as a parish pastor. From the foregoing, we are in a position to draw specific conclusions regarding the influences that shaped his pastoral theology and his unique conception of the moral life.

Edwards's vision for ministry was shaped in important ways by his childhood years in the parsonage. The issues confronted by his father in ministry, including struggles over salary, ministerial authority, and the need for building a new church, all became pressing problems for Edwards's own ministry. Just how these early childhood experiences affected his perceptions of his work are difficult to ascertain. Nevertheless, it seems fair to conclude that his expectations about life in the ministry were formed during this period.

Of deeper significance was the strain of living under the shadow of his maternal grandfather and predecessor, Solomon Stoddard. This situation greatly limited his freedom to fully articulate his own vision for ministry. Only in the later years of his pastoral work at Northampton did he challenge the communion policy of his venerable grandfather. This action came at a time when his own popularity was waning, when the "revival of religion" seems to have had its best days, and when his

---

84. Cited in ibid., 218.

85. From "Christ the Example," preached at the ordination of Job Strong on June 29, 1749 as cited in ibid., 218.

influence as a religious leader in the wider community had become somewhat suspect.

In Edwards's later writings, particularly those produced at Stockbridge during a period of "worldlessness," a recognizable shift occurs in the focus of his writings. Rather than decrying the "debauchery" of Sabbath-breaking, swearing, and smoking in the streets, we find him articulating a vision of the moral life described as, "the consent, propensity and union of heart to Being in general, that is immediately exercised in a general good will." This mindset may be attributed to the freedom he experienced in the Stockbridge location to express his thoughts about the moral life from his own unique perspective. Once out from the shadow of Solomon Stoddard and the pressures of life in the parish at Northampton, he was able to express a positive and wide-ranging vision for the moral life. There is a certain irony in the fact that his best work as a theological ethicist occurred in "exile" while he was ministering among Indians after expulsion from his Northampton parish.

Edwards's experience of conversion is reflected throughout his life work and writings. He maintained a passionate interest in the subtle nuances of the integration of the mind, heart, and will. Borrowing ideas from Lockean psychology, he constructed a view of the affections that surpassed both the intellectualism of Boston and the religious enthusiasm of the revivals of 1734–1735 and 1740–1742, and carefully reflected on the epistemological origins of what he termed, "the sense of the heart." Throughout his life, he refined his vision of the spiritual life, concluding that true religious affections conveyed both "heat" and "light." That is to say that they include both the warming of the spiritual heart and the sharpness of the searching mind.

His increasing clarity about the nature of the spiritual life became a foundation for his last written work, *The Nature of True Virtue*. Here he articulates a vision of virtue that reflects a growing aesthetic theology and an integrative sense of the personal dimensions of the moral life, including natural conscience, the affinities of beauty, and the consent of the will toward a broad ontological scheme of the nature of the world and love for God.

The images for ministry with which Edwards identifies may be seen as compelling scripts informing his pastoral work. These images emphasize his position of delegated authority as Christ's representative in the congregation. He perceived the pastoral charge as a burdensome responsibility that exacted a heavy price, as seen in the example of the "steward" who must give an account to God for the souls that had been entrusted to him. The suffering savior offered a theological explanation for the strains and burdens of his declining popularity in later years at Northampton. Likewise, the voice of the "trumpet," an important sensational image, reflects his sense of responsibility to "influence and affect" those who listen.

In the final chapter I will propose pastoral images that are more congruent with Edwards's vision in *The Nature of True Virtue*. These are *the good Shepherd*, who courageously lays down her life; *the weeping prophet*, who identifies with the affliction of others and expresses the tears of God for those in pain; and *the attentive poet* who listens to the Wind (Hebrew, *ruach*) of God and sensitively articulates the hope of the gospel.

Finally, I have argued that the incongruence between Edwards's private views of the moral life and those required by his public responsibility as a shaper of New England's religious world was resolved only after he left his parish at Northampton. I have suggested that it was during the last period of his life, in Stockbridge, that he found the freedom to express his vision of the moral life as moving away from the rigid moral codes of legislated conduct. I have further suggested that he may have found in his dismissal as pastor at Northampton a new vocation as God's spokesperson, one offering a different and much broader framework for the moral life. He became "worldless" when he was dismissed from his work as parish pastor at Northampton. This experience, however, allowed him to frame his theological perspectives outside of the worldview of the church that had been his from childhood. His expanded expression of the moral life allowed for a fresh and stimulating vision of virtue.

In this chapter, I have laid the groundwork for our exploration, in the next chapter, of the nature of virtue as presented in the current literature, placing these descriptions of the moral life in dialogue with the vision Edwards presented in his dissertation, *The Nature of True Virtue*.

2

Virtue Theory and Edwards's Concept of True Virtue

THE PRIMARY AIM OF this chapter is to demonstrate the value of Jonathan Edwards's concept of true virtue for a pastoral theology of virtue. Many thinkers in the field of theological ethics employ virtue theory as an important development in the general framework of moral philosophy, yet Edwards's idea of virtue remains largely unexamined in the virtue literature. I am proposing that Edwards's conception of virtue uniquely contributes to contemporary discussions of virtue theory and, more specifically, that it may be used as a basis for a constructive vision of virtue in pastoral theology.

I have set myself four tasks in this chapter. First, I will describe some of the dominant features of virtue ethics. This will entail an overview of the current literature in the fields of moral philosophy and theological ethics and a summary of these features of virtue ethics. Second, I will address some possible objections to the use of Edwards's scheme of virtue in current discussions on virtue theory. Third, I will articulate a coherent understanding of Edwards's conception of virtue. Finally, I will offer suggestions concerning the usefulness of Edwards's idea of virtue for a theoretical construct of virtue in pastoral theology.

Turning then to the first of these tasks I wish to articulate some of the more salient features of virtue ethics in the growing body of literature.

FEATURES OF VIRTUE ETHICS

Virtue ethics is an approach to moral philosophy that emphasizes character and human agency in ethics. As such, it must be seen "as a distinct mode of moral philosophy, different from and in competition with the other modes."[1] According to David Solomon, virtue ethics "suggests not only that moral philosophy should 'pay attention' to virtue concepts and include a virtue component in a complete normative theory, but that the concept of virtue is in important respects a more fundamental notion than the concepts of 'the right' or 'the good' where the good is seen as attaching to objects as possible consequences of our action."[2]

One of the difficulties for any investigation of the ethics of virtue is the broad scope of topics and perspectives that are classified as a virtue approach to ethics. Commenting on this difficulty Sarah Conly observes:

> One's first impression on reviewing contemporary literature on virtue is that here, more than most places in philosophy, anything goes. Virtues may be learned like skills, or natural; unreflective desires (such as spontaneous promptings of affection) are considered virtues; introspection and autonomy (presumably arrived at only through reflection) are considered virtues. Virtue may or may not involve acting in accordance with rules one believes in. The virtuous person may or may not have an idea of the good. The desire to do what is right, as such, may be the quintessence of or totally unrelated to virtue.[3]

The discussions in moral philosophy about virtue are not simple and clear cut. They derive from a broad range of reflections on the moral life and have a variety of philosophical agendas. The focus of this section, therefore, will be to expound some of the commonly held features of virtue theory as a distinctive mode of doing ethics. Interacting with both proponents and critics of virtue ethics, I will isolate five distinctive features of this approach. Admittedly, the features selected and outlined here are by no means comprehensive or conclusive, but rather offer a summary of most prominent discussions of virtue theory in moral philosophy.

Virtue Ethics Is Fundamentally "Teleological"

The focus of a "teleological" approach to ethics is on the *telos* (a Greek word) or goal of human nature. The assumption is that in the very fabric of humanity's make-up, there is a thrusting towards some innate end

---

1. Wallace, "Ethics," 222.
2. Solomon, "Internal Objections," 430.
3. Conly, "Flourishing and the Ethics of Virtue," 84.

or telos. The nature of such a goal may be variously defined based on the understanding of human nature, the worldview of the philosopher, and the cultural context from which the person lives. However, the perception that ethics is best defined as a movement towards a goal is an essential feature of most approaches to virtue ethics.

In Aristotle's scheme, for example, the end or goal of human activity is "the good," which is defined as "that at which all things aim."[4] Expanding this view in concentric circles Aristotle concludes "that the good for man is an activity of soul in accordance with virtue, or if there are more kinds of virtue than one, in accordance with the best and most perfect kind."[5] In this scheme, the telos, or goal, of ethics is determined by the pursuit of the good and is indicated by *eudaimonia*, which is translates as "happiness," or better, as "flourishing," which, according to David Jones, attempts "to express in one word Aristotle's complex notion of being good and faring well."[6] In this respect most theories of virtue convey a teleological scheme that looks toward some outcome or aim of the moral life.

It should be noted, however, that not all theories of virtue are teleological. Daniel Statman argues that the traditional deontological/teleological division in ethics is not a useful one for approaches that emphasize virtue. He suggests that while in virtue ethics "the concept of good is prior," it "utilises no notion of maximisation."[7] He argues that, although many writers on virtue ethics defend some sort of teleological view, this emphasis tends to obscure the "unique nature of virtue ethics, because it makes it hard to distinguish between virtue ethics and (a rich notion of) utilitarianism."[8]

While acknowledging that a philosophical ethic need not include a teleological scheme, some ethicists have argued that the use of virtue ethics from a distinctly Christian perspective requires a teleological ethic. This is the force of Kotva's arguments for the use of virtue ethics in the enterprise of Christian theological ethics. Following MacIntyre, he points to the "true nature" of humanity as an essential question of the virtue ethics approach to moral thought. He suggests that "virtue theory

4. Aristotle, *The Nichomachean Ethics*, 63.
5. Ibid., 76.
6. Jones, *Biblical Christian Ethics*, 17.
7. Statman, *Virtue Ethics*, 10.
8. Ibid., 11.

deals with the transition from who we are to who we could be. A concern with this transition requires that we also try to discover our true nature or telos and ascertain our present state or nature."[9]

A more difficult issue for proponents of virtue ethics than the teleological nature of the approach, however, is the lack of consensus on what the particular telos or goal of human flourishing might be. While proponents of virtue theory generally move away from duty-based approaches to ethics, there is very little common agreement concerning the nature of humanity's telos or goal. Critics of the virtue ethics approach cite this inability to define the goal of human flourishing as one of its primary difficulties.

James D. Wallace, for example, argues that while the "craft analogy" (the idea that the achievement of virtue is much like the achievement of other crafts such as medicine, carpentry, or playing a musical instrument)[10] used by virtue ethics may play a significant role in determining the best way to live, the "fixed-goal theory of practical reasoning" must be "abandoned."[11] The fixed-goal approach, says Wallace, fails to offer a precise conception of the telos or goal of the good life that allows for the solving of practical problems. In his view, "the fixed-goal view of practical reasoning . . . places inordinate demands upon our idea of a good life. How, on this view of practical reasoning, are we to decide how the obvious candidates for important human goods are to be fitted together in the good human life?"[12]

In my view, such objections unfairly critique virtue ethics. While it is true that a common consensus of the telos or goal for human living has not been agreed upon by proponents of virtue ethics, the argument

---

9. Kotva, *Christian Case*, 17.

10. Wallace, "Ethics," 223. Wallace explains the craft analogy this way: "What does one need to know to pursue a craft intelligently and successfully? The question can be answered by considering the point or purpose of the activity and the sorts of difficulties its practitioners encounter. The standard according to which the craft is practiced well or badly can be understood in these terms. That healers need to have certain traits and skills can be shown to be true by considering what healers do, what sorts of problems they face in doing it, and what is known about solving these problems. It is obviously true that there are better and worse ways of practicing crafts, and there is no need to invent extraordinary intellectual acts and faculties for apprehending these truths . . . It is plausible to suggest that there are truths about how one should conduct one's life that are known in similar ways."

11. Ibid., 228.

12. Ibid., 227.

that virtue ethics fails to provide criteria for deciding which human goods are to be chosen is problematic. Solomon offers three guiding thoughts to refute this argument. First, an ethics of virtue can guide action more successfully than the objection seems to recognize. Second, the deontological and consequentialist alternatives to an ethics of virtue are less successful at guiding action than the objection alleges. Third, the demand for determinate action-guidingness as spelled out by ethics of virtue opponents involves several dubious claims about the relation between ethical theory and action.[13]

My primary point here is that virtue ethics requires a clearly delineated goal or telos in order to offer the action-guiding decisiveness expected of an ethical theory. While a common agreement on the specifics of the human telos is lacking, Joseph J. Kotva Jr. suggests that some consensus can be achieved on the following:[14]

(a) That the human good or telos is largely constituted by the practice or exercise of various virtues.

(b) That the virtues that lead us to the telos are also components of it, that is, of the best kind of human life.[15]

(c) That the nature of the human good is, at its core, both individual and corporate.

Notably, Alasdair MacIntyre's entire critique of the failure of the enlightenment is based on the shift in moral philosophy away from its teleological foundations.[16]

---

13. Solomon, "Internal Objections," 437 (author's emphasis). I refer the reader to this excellent article for a thorough response to objections raised against virtue ethics.

14. See discussion by Kotva, *Christian Case*, 20–21.

15 This is Kotva's response to the argument that virtue ethics is non-teleological. Kotva argues: "Some authors reject the label 'teleological,' not because they reject virtue theory's need for a conception of the human good, but because 'teleological' suggests to them an end external to, and ultimately independent of, the virtues." The view he advances, with which I am in sympathy, "views the virtues as both leading to and constituting the human telos." Kotva, *Christian Case*, 21.

16 After evaluating Pascal, Kant, Hume, Smith, Diderot, and Kierkegaard, MacIntyre concludes, "All reject any teleological view of human nature, any view of man as having an essence which defines his true end. But to understand this is to understand why their project of finding a basis for morality had to fail." Continuing this important argument he adds, "Hence the eighteenth-century moral philosophers engaged in what was an inevitably unsuccessful project; for they did indeed attempt to find a rational basis for their moral beliefs in a particular understanding of human nature, while inheriting a set

Virtue Ethics Emphasizes Human Agency and Character

Virtue ethics emphasizes the agency of human persons bearing traits or "virtues" over the rules and principles that might guide the moral life. This feature of virtue ethics allows it to offer a wider scope of reflection on the nuances of the moral life. As Solomon points out, because the virtues "embody a more complex capacity for discernment than do rules and principles, they defy formulation in rules or principles."[17] Thus, the central moral question for virtue ethics is not, "What should I do?" but "What sort of person am I to be?" States of character and the acquisition of the virtues are given priority over concern with specific choices. Virtue ethics recognizes that "who I become" will inform and determine my choices and actions.

It is not that virtue ethics is unconcerned with specific choices or moral quandaries as has sometimes been argued. Rather, virtue ethics recognizes that character formation predisposes us to act and respond in certain ways. A just person will act justly, and a benevolent person will respond to a plight with generosity, and so on. As Kotva asserts:

> Virtue ethics' concern with virtues and vices is not viewed as lack of concern for right action. It is, rather, the realization that right action, right judgment, and rightly ordered character are intimately linked. Indeed, the ability to determine and do the right is premised on one's having the requisite states of character.[18]

Thus virtue theory understands the function of character as the basis for the moral life. Character formation and the inculcation of the virtues have precedence over the establishment of rules for society. The primacy given to character distinguishes virtue ethics from other theories of the moral life.

According to Daniel Statman, virtue ethics reverses the paradigm in duty ethics from actions to virtues and from principles to character. In virtue ethics, "aretaic judgments, i.e. judgments about character, are prior to deontic judgments, i.e., judgment about the rightness or wrongness of actions."[19] Virtue ethics therefore provides a corrective to normative

---

of moral injunctions on the one hand and a conception of human nature on the other which had been expressly designed to be discrepant with each other." MacIntyre, *After Virtue*, 54–55.

17 MacIntrye, *After Virtue*, 439.

18. Kotva, *Christian Case*, 30.

19. Statman, *Virtue Ethics*, 8.

ethics by centering on the person and her character rather than debates about moral norms, ethical maxims, and prevailing principles, debates that often leave participants unconvinced by one another's arguments.

While not exclusively interested in the cultivation of individual moral formation, virtue ethics has the merit of at least recognizing the moral formation of persons as an important dimension of the moral life. It seeks to ground the work of ethics in the day-to-day formation of persons in society and in the realistic assessment that progress, if it can be measured at all in the moral life, takes place in the lives of persons.

Virtue Ethics Heightens Moral Vision

Moral vision, or the ability to articulate a moral situation with clarity, is an important feature of the virtue ethics approach. Virtue ethics uses the imagery of vision to express the nuances of perception that are regarded as important aspects of moral understanding. To quote an important proponent of virtue theory, Gilbert Meilaender:

> An ethic of virtue is dominated by the eye, by metaphors of sight and vision. To know what traits of character qualify as virtues we must see our world and human nature rightly. To see rightly, in turn, requires that we have the virtues. Virtue enhances *vision*; vice darkens and finally *blinds*.[20]

The mutuality of vision and virtue is an important feature of this approach to ethics. An adequate virtue ethic will discover ways to heighten moral vision and will, likewise, reflect an urgency concerning issues of character development that assist in one's ability to perceive a moral problem. The understanding that character determines what we see is important for advocates of a virtue ethic. Our perceptions of a moral situation are not based only on reason or duty, as other approaches suggest, but on who we are in the moral situation. Character determines how we perceive a moral situation.

Moral vision is further heightened in the virtue ethics approach by its ability to isolate specific nuances of the moral life. Solomon notes that "contemporary moral philosophers pay excessive attention to the most abstract terms involved in ethical thought and talk, terms like 'right,' 'good,' and 'ought,' while largely ignoring richer and more concrete terms

---

20. Meilaender, *Theory and Practice*, 17 (author's emphasis).

like 'sensitive,' 'compassionate,' and 'courageous.'"[21] Thus, by attending to these subtle nuances, virtue ethics allows for a more complete expression of the moral life, and the richness and depth of the language of the virtues allows for a broader discussion of the complexities of the moral life. Just as the primary colors find their expression in many subtle shades and refractions of light, so too the moral life cannot be reduced to a set of laws or moral principles but is rather a complex rainbow of lived virtues.

Moral vision and expression of that vision through language are the unique emphases of virtue ethics. How we perceive the moral situation has to do in large part with who we are as moral agents. The complexities of the moral situation are not merely problems to be worked out in relationship to principles of ethical responsibility, but rather require the discernment of subtle shifts in the moral landscape, eliciting something in us that is attentive to our purpose as agents of moral participation.

This also means that moral blindness, the inability to see a moral situation with clarity, is connected to the issue of virtue. As Iris Murdoch notes:

> By opening our eyes we do not necessarily see what confronts us. We are anxiety-ridden animals. Our minds are continually active, fabricating an anxious, usually self-preoccupied, often falsifying veil which partially conceals the world . . . And if quality of consciousness matters, then anything which alters consciousness in the direction of unselfishness, objectivity and realism is to be connected with virtue.[22]

The interior condition of the human agent is therefore an important feature of virtue ethics. It allows for the dynamic interplay of the inner character of the person and the social fabric with which the moral life is concerned.

Virtue Ethics Correlates All of the Virtues

A common theme in discussions about virtue is the relationship of the individual virtues to virtue as a whole. Are the virtues to be considered as a unity? Are there certain unifying virtues from which all the others are

---

21. Solomon, "Internal Objections," 428. This article is also included in Statman, *Virtue Ethics*, 165.

22. Murdoch, *Sovereignty of Good*, 84.

derived? Since Augustine, Christian theology has generally assumed the unity of the virtues. Writing to St. Jerome in AD 415, Augustine notes: "He who has one virtue has them all, and he who does not have a particular one has none . . . Prudence can be neither cowardly, nor unjust, nor intemperate, for if it is any of these it will not be prudence."[23] Traditional discussions about virtue center on the four "cardinal virtues"—justice, wisdom (prudence), courage (fortitude), and moderation (self-control, temperance), and the three "theological virtues"—faith, hope, and charity.[24] These, it is thought, provide the focal points for discussions of all the auxiliary virtues.

Consensus regarding the unity of the virtues has, however, been elusive. While Amelie O. Rorty articulates a common impression with the statement, "the virtues hunt in packs,"[25] discovering the way the virtues are ordered is no simple task. Meilaender suggests that one's conclusion regarding the unity of the virtues will be guided by one's sense of the structure of the moral life itself. He argues:

> If we are impressed primarily with the tragic choices often encountered in the moral life, we are likely to believe that the many virtues are not one—that someone may well be courageous in an unjust cause, temperate (even a great ascetic) while torturing the innocent, and so forth. If, on the other hand, we are impressed primarily with the fact that judgments of character are made, finally, not upon isolated virtues or vices but upon persons, we are likely to believe that the many virtues are one—that any defect in virtue must to some extent permeate and corrupt the entire self, leaving only seeming virtues or splendid vices.[26]

While unable to solve decisively the exact interplay of the virtues, the strength of virtue ethics is its characteristic attempt to articulate the good life in all of its complexity.[27] In the virtue approach to ethics there is a sense of the dynamic interaction of the virtues in the formation of character. Character becomes the framework from which virtue is understood and from which the moral life is delineated.

---

23. Langan, "Augustine on the Unity," 84–85.
24. See Kreeft, *Back to Virtue*, 59–78; cf. Cessario, *Moral Virtues*, 1–18.
25. Rorty, "Virtues," 137.
26. Meilaender, *Theory and Practice*, 22.
27. For a thorough and thoughtful discussion of the interplay of the virtues on each other and the various theories in that regard, see Rorty, "Virtues."

Virtue Ethics Conceives the Moral Life in Community

The perception that virtue ethics inordinately focuses on the individual is misguided. One common consensus in virtue approaches to ethics is the understanding that the shaping of character takes place in community. Community is the context for the development of character. A consistent theme in virtue ethics is the understanding that character is not shaped in a social vacuum but that the moral life is formed as we participate in the wider community. Although virtue ethics has its eye on the interior functions of the moral life (virtues), the exterior context in which a person lives shapes and gives meaning to that moral life. Rorty expands this perspective: "Action takes place in a social world. It is, in the end, our social and political relation to others that keeps our virtues in whatever precariously appropriate balance they have . . . Significantly, our actions have their sense, their meaning, and their direction in a public, interactive world."[28]

The social dimension in virtue ethics is seen, for example, in the importance attributed to modeling and imitation in the development of a morally formed life. Moral exemplars are an important feature in many virtue ethics discussions. In this regard Statman concludes: "Becoming a good person [in virtue ethics] is not a matter of learning or applying 'principles,' but of imitating some models . . . According to virtue ethics, education through moral exemplars is more effective than education focused on principles and obligations, because it is far more concrete."[29]

The arguments for imitating a moral exemplar allow virtue ethics to function within the normal sphere of moral development and to focus on the ways in which the character is formed within the community. Although recognizing the complexities of moral formation, virtue ethics is interested in grounding discussions about the good life in concrete interactions between human persons. Seen in this way, the development of the virtuous life is understood as the gradual impression of the human character through active participation in the community. Modeling is seen as an important feature of educating the moral life. Hence, as Alderman points out, "one learns to be virtuous the same way one learns

---

28. Ibid., 144.
29. Statman, *Virtue Ethics*, 13.

to cook, dance, play football and so forth and that is by imitating people who are good at those sorts of things."[30]

The community is the context in which the virtues are developed. The virtuous life reflects the habits, dispositions, and values of the wider community and in turn shapes the wider community as a "community of virtue." For Kotva, this understanding of the person shaped in community requires virtue ethics to offer a conception of the moral life that balances behaviorism and voluntarism. He suggests that "virtue theory assumes that we are embodied creatures whose choices and actions are neither completely determined nor completely free... Today's virtue ethics cannot, any more than Aristotle, be content with reducing all human actions to external causes or to a self free from body, history, and beliefs."[31]

The agent's intentionality is characterized as primary in virtue ethics; however, such intentions are influenced and shaped by the community. Rorty expresses the idea that the balanced pattern of virtues is "co-produced" in much the same way. In this view "character... regulates the particular virtues; and community regulates character."[32]

Summary

Virtue ethics is a viable approach to modern moral theory, especially moral theory that seeks to renew ethics as a fundamentally teleological enterprise. Its focus on character, virtues, and the internal formation of persons and societies grounds it in the real situation of persons and responsibilities rather than in the abstract notions of rules and procedures. Virtue ethics recognizes the need for individuals to grow to maturity and offers strategies for this to happen while moving beyond the concerns of the individual toward the establishing of virtuous communities. It recognizes the interplay between freedom and determinism that is part of living as an embodied person in the community. Virtue theory allows for the nuances of ethical debate to be discerned through practical involvement rather than by moral reasoning alone. It does not ignore rules or principles but focuses the ethical towards the formation of human persons who possess freedom and who are limited. Virtue eth-

---

30. Alderman, "By Virtue of a Virtue," 156.
31. Kotva, *Christian Case*, 27.
32. Rorty, "Virtues," 145.

ics seeks to articulate its vision for the moral life and allows persons to recognize and perceive moral situations with a wider scope of clarity than other rule-oriented ethical theories. Virtue ethics is not stagnant or abstract but engages the entire person in her world in such a way as to encourage and foster the development of virtues and to dissuade and discourage the progress of vice. It realistically moves into the life situation of persons and communities, allowing for strategic change to happen according to an interpretation of human flourishing, a telos that defines the path from humans-as-we-are to humans-as-we might-be.

OBJECTIONS TO THE USE OF JONATHAN EDWARDS'S THEOLOGY OF VIRTUE

Before moving from this description of virtue ethics to Edwards's concept of virtue, I wish to respond to three possible objections that might be made against this approach. The first is that the context of eighteenth-century religious thought may be an inadequate philosophical starting point for deliberation on the current debates in virtue ethics. The second is that there is a lack of literature supporting virtue as a theological theme in general. The third concerns the problems of connecting theology, virtue ethics, and pastoral theology.

Regarding the objection that the context of eighteenth-century religious thought may be an inadequate philosophical starting point, the choice of Jonathan Edwards as a resource for modern reflection in virtue ethics may be criticized both for its religious basis and its distance from the modern context. This is an important critique that warrants a response, but when one considers the vast dimensions of Edwardsean thought, it soon becomes clear that such a criticism fails to take seriously the integrated theological system that he developed in his short life. Though known popularly for his famous sermon, *Sinners in the Hands of an Angry God*, he is also being recognized as one of the great theological minds of America. It is important to note, first, that his extrapolation of the nature of virtue is argued primarily in the context of eighteenth-century philosophical debate rather than as a religious treatise targeting his own congregation. As was seen in the previous chapter, by the time he wrote *True Virtue* he had been exiled from his position as a prominent pastor at Northampton. His new work in the mission outpost allowed him to develop his writing in ways that were not possible in the parish context. One project that had to be set aside, but was evident from his early academic formation, was the development of a conception of the moral life, including natural conscience. The treatise on *The Nature of True Virtue* is a philosophical treatise that is consistent with the theological positions he had systematically expounded throughout his life.

Regarding its philosophical basis and intent, Paul Ramsey's disagreement with Norman Fiering's assertion that Edwards wrote *True Virtue* as a response to Francis Hutcheson is relevant.[33] Ramsey writes: "Edwards' references to Francis Hutcheson in later entries in his 'Miscellanies'... do not support the notion that his principal aim in writing *True Virtue* was to refute Scottish 'moral sense' philosophy."[34] While Edwards had certainly read Hutcheson and made three notations in his writings concerning his views, his vision for a thesis on the moral life may be traced to his early reading of Locke. As Sang Hyan Lee argues, it was his appropriation of Locke's simple idea that formed the philosophical basis of his treatise on virtue:

> The Cambridge Platonists, especially Cudworth and Shaftesbury, undoubtedly inspired Edwards with their insistence upon the important contribution that the mind itself makes to the knowledge process. But their epistemologies had not paid enough attention to the Lockean empiricism to suit Edwards. Edwards' grappling with the Lockean problem resulted in his theories of the imagination and of aesthetic perception—what Edwards called the "sense of the heart"—and here again the idea of habit is the key.[35]

In light of his concern to grapple with the Lockean problem, Edwards's contribution to virtue theory was an important philosophical synthesis, one that has much to contribute to the current debates in moral philosophy and theological ethics. Given its philosophical and theological sophistication, its current revival is most timely. This is particularly true in light of Alasdair MacIntyre's view that modern moral philosophy is at a crossroads. He argues that modern moral philosophy has become post-theistic. This situation creates a vacuum in moral thought since most moral arguments have a theistic heritage. Even if moral philosophers ignore this historical situation, the problem of grounding a moral judgment in some higher law still exists. Precisely this problem results in the impasses common to modern moral philosophy. He concludes,

33. Ramsey, *Ethical Writings*, Appendix II, 689–705.
34. Ibid., 689. Byrnes, "Niebuhr's Reconstruction," 44.
35. Lee, *Philosophical Theology*, 13.

"And it is perhaps this failure to recognize how much of the 'ordinary language' of contemporary morality is a survival from theism that underlies a corresponding failure to reckon with the fact that each of these two alternatives embodies a different kind of moral project."[36]

The value of Edwards's contribution to virtue theory is reflected in the fact that, as Thomas A. Byrnes points out, H. Richard Niebuhr's *The Responsible Self* may be understood as a reconstruction of Edwards's moral theology in *The Nature of True Virtue*.[37] Though recognizing the significant changes of philosophical context from Edwards to Niebuhr, Byrnes contends that their conclusions are the same, namely, that "moral excellency consists in first properly relating oneself to the world in its wholeness and then relating oneself to other beings in a manner appropriate to the part of the role which each plays in that whole."[38] Byrnes also notes that the core of Niebuhr's argument in *The Responsible Self*[39] is actually a reconstruction of Edwards's position, as it replaces Edwards's notion of "beauty" with "the law of my integrity" as the guiding idea for moral theology.

Thus, Edwards's concept of true virtue offers a unique theological voice to the renewed contemporary interest in virtue theory. In light of the most recent attempts in theology to enter into dialogue with moral philosophers, renewed examination of Edwards's concept of virtue is both appropriate and potentially valuable.

The objection that there is a lack of literature supporting virtue as a theological theme in general certainly has significant merits. Cursory study of the biblical record indicates that virtue does not play a significant role in the Scriptures and may even seem contradictory to common theological themes such as grace, redemption, and traditional formulations of theological concepts such as justification and sanctification. How can a theory that relies so heavily on human agency include such important theological motifs? Can it not be said that virtue theory, by its

---

36. MacIntyre, "Moral Philosophy," 8.
37. Byrnes, "Niebuhr's Reconstruction."
38. Ibid., 44.
39. Byrnes actually cites the central three chapters of Niebuhr's book and their titles: "Responsibility in Society," "The Responsible Self in Time and History," and "Responsibility in Absolute Dependence," noting that these culminate with Niebuhr's statement of his fundamental moral norm, "the law of my integrity." Byrnes, "Niebuhr's Reconstruction," 46.

very nature, fails to recognize the fundamental posture of humanity as dependent on God for goodness?

The problem with this line of reasoning is that it fails to acknowledge the fact that all cultures and religions seek to offer a meaningful expression of what is good and how it might be achieved. If the Christian perspective is to be relevant in this regard, it must not only participate in the discussion about virtue but offer a distinctive understanding of how virtue is to be understood and cultivated in the lives of people and societies.

There are other considerations here too. If Christian theology expresses God as the source of all goodness,[40] then a systematic investigation of that theology would imply a theory of virtue. Only recently have theologians returned, after a long hiatus, to an understanding of virtue from a biblical and theological perspective. This new development is an improvement to the dialogue with all who search for moral insight in our world. God's goodness must continue to serve as a catalyst for understanding the nature of virtue itself and the moral posture of humanity in relationship with God.

It should also be noted that, although reference to virtue in particular may be lacking in the Scriptures, the general concern for moral formation and integrity stand at the heart of both the Old and New Testaments. Benjamin W. Farley explores the fabric of virtue in the Scriptures in *In Praise of Virtue*. Though cautious about embracing a virtue ethic as a basis for anthropology, he systematically identifies, explores, and reflects on the virtues indicated in both the Old and New Testaments.

In Hebrew thought the essential expectations of Yahweh with his people are conveyed in moral-ethical terms: "He has shown you, O man, what is good; and what does the Lord require of you but to do justice, to love kindness, and to walk humbly with your God? "(Mic 6:8). This and many other defining texts of the Old Testament express God's desire for humanity to live virtuously before him. What is good? The Old Testament claims that the good is justice, kindness, and humility. The

---

40. Arguing for the Christian vision of virtue in Aquinas, for example, Benjamin W. Farley articulates an essential understanding in both Protestant and Catholic theology that virtue is rooted in God's character: "But Aquinas goes beyond Aristotle and grounds the virtues in the Godhead: They, says Aquinas, 'pre-exist in God as exemplars.' Wisdom is the Divine Mind; temperance is God gazing 'only on Himself'; courage is God's 'unchangeableness'; and justice is God's 'obedience of the Eternal Law.'" Farley, *In Praise of Virtue*, 19.

language of the virtues and the expressed agenda of the virtuous life lie behind the entire fabric of the covenant relationship of God and his people in the Old Testament.

The same may be said for the New Testament. If Jesus' own vision for humanity is seen as paradigmatic for his disciples (the Greek word translated "disciple" is *mathetes*—one who learns) then the Beatitudes might summarize the life of true virtue: to be poor in spirit, to mourn rightly, to live with gentleness, to be full of mercy, to be pure in heart, making peace with others, being steadfast under persecution. These descriptive summaries of the authentic life of one who follows Christ may be seen as a broader paradigm for the life of virtue.

Similarly, the epistles mark out the life of virtue with lists of qualities to be inculcated in the life of the believing person. Such lists abound in the New Testament. Take, for example, the fruit of the life led by God's Spirit indicated in the epistle to the Galatians: "But the fruit of the Spirit is love, joy, peace, patience, kindness, goodness, faithfulness, gentleness, self control; against such things there is no law" (Gal 5:22). Each of these biblical citations encourages various virtues and expressly understands the maturing Christian life as the life that has embraced the pursuit of these character traits. Thus, even a brief overview of biblical thought indicates that the pursuit of virtue is a primary aim of the life that pleases God. Recognition of this biblical emphasis gives credence to the effort to develop a more full and Christian interpretation of virtue ethics.

The third objection concerning the interdisciplinary approach of this project, specifically its concern to relate theology, virtue ethics, and pastoral theology, must also be addressed. With the varied assumptions of distinctively separate disciplines such as systematic theology, virtue ethics, and pastoral theology, how might the methodological problems encountered be resolved? This is a particular problem for my work, in that I have chosen Edward's concept of virtue as the theoretical construct of virtue for pastoral theology.

Three favorable conditions make this challenging task plausible. First, Edwards's treatise is precisely concerned to articulate a view of virtue. He is not extrapolating an understanding of sanctification, or justice, or some other related theological theme, and then associating it with moral theology. He is rather unfolding a specifically Christian vision of virtue, a philosophical treatise on the nature of true virtue. If he is successful in his attempt to define virtue both philosophically and theologically, then his work is particularly suited to the dialogical nature of the current project.

Second, Edwards is particularly suited to this triad from his own lifetime achievements; he distinguished himself as a formidable theologian, a devoted pastor, and a perceptive philosopher. Significantly, he began and ended his career, not as a minister, but as a theological educator. His tutorship at Yale and his presidency at Princeton serve as bookends to his life in service in the church. Likewise his commitment to his congregation, despite obstacles and misunderstandings, resulted in a pastoral tenure of over twenty-two years. His contributions to theology are still being explored to this day, with more than fifteen major theological treatises in his corpus of writings. He seems an excellent candidate for this project based on his own life achievements.

A third reason for the advancement of this project is the potential contribution that his treatise has for modern virtue ethics. Few theologians have articulated a clear and precise theory of virtue. As one who has contributed a voice to this discussion, Edwards offers an important perspective from which to examine modern theological approaches to the concept of virtue, thereby contributing significantly to the growing body of literature that approaches virtue ethics from a distinctively Christian perspective.

Thus, in my judgment, the philosophical theology of Jonathan Edwards has a good fit with the particular triad of theology, virtue theory, and pastoral theology, and the enterprise in which I am engaged here promises a significant contribution to the growing literature in virtue ethics from a distinctively Christian perspective.

JONATHAN EDWARDS'S CONCEPT OF TRUE VIRTUE

I turn now to the specific content of Edwards's construction of virtue in *The Nature of True Virtue*. In this section I focus on the contribution that a theological conception of virtue may make to the general advancement of virtue ethics and outline some of the specific features that make Edwards's conception of virtue particularly valuable to this enterprise.

In order to unpack his treatise, it is important to recognize that Edwards was formulating a conception of virtue that may be described as an aesthetic theology. His aim was to convey a sense of true "beauty" that forms a basis for ethics. For him, beauty "does not consist in discord and dissent, but in consent and agreement."[41] These two concepts of "consent" and "agreement" are key terms in the articulation of his theory of moral virtue. Once consent is identified as the method of appropriating true virtue, it is a matter of course for Edwards to conclude that the object of true affection must be the greatest object: "When viewed most perfectly, comprehensively and universally, with regard to all its tendencies, and its connections with every thing to which it stands related."[42]

Edwards cannot speak of virtues that are separated from this universal object of love, for such actions fall short of true virtue, that is, they fail to relate to everything with which they stand connected. Thus, true virtue always exercises its affection for the greatest, most comprehensive and universal Beauty. Ultimately, this means "inclining to the general highest good"[43] and "love to God; the Being of beings, infinitely the greatest and best."[44]

True virtue, then, is consent to "being in general"[45] measured by "agreeableness."[46] As Edwards explains:

> For the true virtue of created beings is doubtless their highest excellency, and their true goodness, and that by which they are especially agreeable to the mind of their Creator. But the true goodness of a thing must be its agreeableness to its end, or its fitness to answer the design for which it was made.[47]

Edwards articulates moral agency in terms of the purpose or telos of humanity. We are created to be moral agents and, to the extent that we "agree" with God about our design, we move towards our ultimate purpose. We express this agreement through consent to Being in general. The concept of agreement here must not be minimized as being some character trait or quality of human response. It is rather of the nature of true virtue to "agree" or offer "consent" to "being in general." Edwards

---

41. Ibid., 4.
42. Ibid., 3.
43. Ibid., 9.
44. Ibid., 14.
45. Ibid., 8.
46. Ibid., 24.
47. Ibid., 25.

understands this as a function of human agency within the entire scheme of reality.

This leads to Edwards's concept of virtue ethics:

> The first object of a virtuous benevolence is being simply considered; and if being, simply considered, be its object, then being in general is its object; and what it has an ultimate propensity to is the highest good of being in general. And it will seek the good of every individual being unless it be conceived as not consistent with the highest good of being in general.[48]

Here he begins to shift from his aesthetic theology of agreement with beauty to a practical conception of virtue as the propensity to "the highest good of being in general" and the seeking of "the good of every individual being." There is a subtle nuance between "seeking" and "propensity." This is the style of argument he employs throughout his treatise. Our "propensity" in virtue must be to "being in general," or to what he terms elsewhere in the treatise as "general beauty." Only if this first condition of virtue is met can we begin to think about moral actions toward other created beings and "seek" their good. General beauty must be apprehended before particular beauty can find its context.

Key Concepts in Jonathan Edwards's Construct of Virtue

My aim, to this point, has been to show the general texture of Edwards's thought in developing his theology of virtue. As has been stated, it is evident that his concept of virtue has the promise of adding a unique theological voice to current discussions in moral philosophy and ethics on the theme of virtue. I now proceed to a more nuanced discussion of the treatise. To show the usefulness of his moral scheme for a pastoral theology of virtue I will explore some important terms and his use of them.[49] Though there are many important distinctions in this complex work, I highlight three that explicitly relate to this project of understanding his concept of true virtue. These are being, beauty, and consent.

---

48. Ibid., 8.

49. My indebtedness to many Edwards's scholars will be most evident through this section. Among the primary interpreters of Edwards that I follow here are: Lee, *Philosophical Theology*; Delattre, *Beauty and Sensibility*; Ramsey, *Ethical Writings*; Holbrook, *Ethics of Jonathan Edwards*; Simonson, *Jonathan Edwards*.

Being

As I have shown, if virtue ethics prioritizes "being" over "doing" in its overarching scheme, then one structural component of a theological construct of virtue will necessarily be ontological, i.e., an expressed understanding of the nature of being itself. Edwards's understanding of virtue certainly fits this requirement in that his entire argument rests on the concept of "benevolence" to being. His most common reference in *The Nature of True Virtue* is to "being in general." For Edwards, true virtue always must take "being in general" as its frame of reference. He develops two strains of thought simultaneously, slipping regularly from discussions about "being in general" to statements about "God as the supreme being." Thus, his treatise may be considered (a) an ontological argument for the nature of virtue as consent to being in general and (b) a theological argument for the centrality of God in the way the universe is structured.[50]

Edwards's complex idea of being expresses more than one first imagines. This complexity is identified by Sang Hyun Lee in *The Philosophical Theology of Jonathan Edwards*. Lee describes Edwards's ontological structure of reality as essentially "relational." Key to this argument is Edwards's contention that "the universe is the external expression and repetition of God's internal being."[51] Thus, when he speaks of consent to "being in general" he has in mind precisely this relational notion of God's infinite repetition of God's character in time and space. True virtue is most specifically related to this objective reality in the sentient being's consent or agreement with being in general. The relationship between God's infinite self-expression in time and space and true virtue cannot be overstated. From his early encounter with God at his conversion, he was looking for words that might describe his experience of God's splendor and majesty breaking into the world.

In this treatise Edwards has achieved what he had attempted to express in a lifetime, namely, an understanding of the ontological structure

---

50. Others share this assessment. Consider, for example, the statement by Roland Andre Delattre: "Edwards builds up this position both philosophically and theologically: (a) philosophically, in terms of a dynamic dispositional philosophy of being . . . and (b) theologically in terms of a thoroughly trinitarian theory of the internal life of God *ad intra* as well as of God's self-communication *ad extra* in the creation and redemption of the world." Delattre, "Theological Ethics," 77.

51. Lee, *Philosophical Theology*, 81.

of the universe as God's character repeated in time and space. The moral component of this relational ontology is that by our benevolence to "being in general" (which is the equivalent of God's infinite self-expression in time and space) we, as intelligent, sentient beings, act according to the nature of true virtue. Thus, for Edwards, it is our regard for "being in general," rather than the limited sphere of our own private affections, that determines the degree to which our actions are of the nature of true virtue. This wider regard is of focal concern in Edwards's ethical scheme. He writes: "For he that is influenced by private affection, not subordinate to a regard to being in general, sets up its particular or limited object above being in general."[52]

Lee calls this "the doctrine of the whole,"[53] and goes on to identify three important elements of this doctrine. The first is that "what an entity is, is inseparable from its relations."[54] That is, "in Edwards' ontology, relations are internal to being . . . Being is being-in-relation."[55] Second, "relations determine the existence of an entity."[56] Thus, "not only the what-ness of an entity but also its that-ness is constituted by relations."[57] Third, Edwards insists on "the absolutely comprehensive extent of the mutual relations of all entities."[58] Lee concludes that "entities are related not only with some other entities in the system of being but with *all* other entities—that is, with the whole."[59] Precisely this integrated relational ontology is at the heart of all Edwardsean thought.[60]

BEAUTY

I have stated that Edwards's theory of virtue may be described as an aesthetic theology. This view derives from the outset of his treatise where, in describing the conditions for true virtue, Edwards points to beauty

---

52. Edwards, *True Virtue*, 20.
53. Lee, *Philosophical Theology*, 82.
54. Ibid., 77.
55. Ibid., 78.
56. Ibid., 79.
57. Ibid.
58. Ibid., 80.
59. Ibid. (emphasis his).
60. Note Ramsey's editorial comment: "It is a grave error, now or ever, to separate Edwards' philosophy from his theology, or his moral philosophy from his theological ethics." Ramsey, *Ethical Writings*, 11.

as the starting point. He begins with the rather vague and undefined premise that "whatever controversies and variety of opinions there are about the nature of virtue, yet all excepting some sceptics, who deny any real difference between virtue and vice, mean by it something beautiful, or rather some kind of beauty or excellency."[61]

From the outset, therefore, Edwards's idea of virtue is tied to the concept of beauty. Roland Delattre points to the importance of this feature in Edwards's thought:

> If we wish to understand and appreciate Edwards we must dare to take seriously his frequent suggestions that beauty is the central clue to the nature of reality. We must pursue the possibility that the aesthetic aspect of his thought and vision . . . his concept of beauty is primarily objective, structural, and relational rather than subjective, emotional, and relativist.[62]

Beauty, for Edwards, is divisible into two principal types: *primary beauty* and *secondary beauty*. With this distinction he relates the moral life of the "spiritual" (primary beauty) with that of the "natural" (secondary beauty). Primary beauty is the beauty "of spiritual and moral beings, which are the highest and first part of the universal system."[63] All union and consent with being in general, insofar as it takes into account the universal scheme, is entailed in this quality of primary beauty. Primary beauty involves the moral sense and what Edwards terms "cordial consent" or "cordial agreement." Accordingly, the "consent, agreement, or union of being to being" that is "the union or propensity of minds to mental or spiritual existence, may be called the highest and primary beauty."[64]

Delattre sees a parallel between Edwards's concept of primary beauty and Alfred North Whitehead's distinction between the major and minor forms of beauty. He cites the role of beauty in Whitehead's metaphysics and theology: "All order is . . . aesthetic order, and the moral order is merely certain aspects of aesthetic order. The actual world is the

---

61. Edwards, *True Virtue*, 1.

62. Delattre, "Beauty and Theology," 136, 137. Delattre also draws this conclusion on the basis of Richard R. Niebuhr's observation that "the foundation of his [Edwards's] ontology, of his philosophy of being, lies in proportionality or in complex, intense beauty. In fact, Edwards' ethics is founded on this conviction as well." Niebuhr is cited by Delattre in "Theological Ethics," 85.

63. Edwards, *True Virtue*, 27.

64. Ibid.

outcome of the aesthetic order, and the aesthetic order is derived from the immanence of God."[65] The striking parallel in both schemes is the concept that the moral order is derived from the aesthetic order. For Edwards, there is an intimate connection between primary beauty and true virtue. Primary beauty is "the 'consent' (love) between perceiving beings,"[66] which is essentially "spiritual (mental)."[67]

Secondary beauty is the form that usually comes to mind when we think of something being beautiful. This "natural" beauty has to do with symmetry, proportion, uniformity, and harmony. As Paul Ramsey states, "Edwards observed beauty in the symmetry of buildings, in melodies, and in the infinite number of equalities in a rose, a countenance, or the solar system."[68] Secondary beauty, says Edwards,

> is not peculiar to spiritual beings, but is found even in inanimate things; which consists in a mutual consent and agreement of different things, in form, manner, quantity, and visible end or design; called by the various names of regularity, order, uniformity, symmetry, proportion, harmony, etc.[69]

This secondary beauty then has to do with the "natural (material) dimensions of reality"[70] which are also tied to the relational ontology described in the previous section. Lee explains:

> When Edwards speaks about the images and types from the natural world, he is not merely coming up with the corporeal illustrations or analogies of certain spiritual meanings; rather he is pointing to all of the dimensions of the relations that make up the very essence of the being of material objects themselves.[71]

Consent

I have already alluded to the fact that consent is the important link between Edwards's ideas of beauty and the nature of true virtue. Consent and its counterpart, dissent, are activities of thinking, willing, feeling

---

65. Whitehead, *Religion in the Making*, 101.
66. Lee, *Philosophical Theology*, 83.
67. Ibid., 83.
68. Ramsey, "Splendor," 7.
69. Edwards, *True Virtue*, 28.
70. Lee, *Philosophical Theology*, 83.
71. Ibid., 88, 89.

persons. The degree of consent or dissent towards being in general is the functional measure of the degree of virtue. This link is described by Delattre as the connection between the aesthetic concept of beauty and the objective relations of consent:

> Beauty is objective for Edwards because it is constituted by objective relations of consent and dissent among beings, relations into which the subject or beholder may enter and participate, but relations the beauty of which is defined by conformity to God (consent to being in general) rather than by degree of subjective pleasure. Beauty is, in other words, a structural concept, the nearest synonym for which is excellence rather than pleasantness.[72]

The concept of consent connects Edwards's aesthetic vision of reality with his ethics. He identifies two forms of consent that parallel the two forms of beauty: "cordial agreement" and "natural agreement."[73] The first parallels primary beauty, as "the cordial or heart-felt consent of being to being."[74] It is precisely here that Edwards offers his definition of "true virtue." "True virtue most essentially consists in benevolence to being in general. Or perhaps, to speak more accurately, it is that consent, propensity and union of heart to being in general, which is immediately exercised in a general good will."[75] Conceived this way, virtue may be understood as an aesthetic correspondent to the nature of reality. The "sensation" of primary or spiritual beauty consists in "a spiritual union and agreement"[76] that goes beyond natural beauty. Thus, true virtue occurs when our hearts are united with God's infinite self-expression through consent and spiritual union, through agreement with God.

Edwards uses this view of true virtue to distinguish between "natural" conceptions of virtue (justice, wisdom, gratitude, etc.) and the "cordial agreement" that unites one's "heart to being in general, or to God, the being of beings."[77] For him, true virtue as primary beauty always means a union of heart to God and a perception of God's infinite self-repetition in time and space. All lesser forms of agreement and harmony are not of the nature of true virtue but are forms of secondary beauty. This

72. Delattre, "Beauty and Theology," 139.
73. Edwards, *True Virtue*, 31.
74. Ibid., 138.
75. Ibid., 3.
76. Ibid., 33.
77. Ibid., 38.

description of virtue allows him to conceive differences in the moral perception of regenerate (primary beauty) and unregenerate (secondary beauty) persons. He does not disparage the sense of moral apprehension that comes with natural agreement but relates this to the intuitive sense of natural conscience. Natural conscience is common to all humanity and "approves" the uniformity, equality, etc. of virtue while being unable to "taste" the "sweetness in benevolence to being in general."[78]

For Edwards, those ethical systems that fail to relate to the "sum of universal being, or comprehending all existence to which we stand related" are flawed primarily by their "narrowness" and in particular, by their readiness "to leave the divine Being out of their view."[79] The breadth of one's moral vision thus depends on one's ability to incorporate God's being (as the Being of beings) into one's way of perceiving the world. Ethical systems that fail in this regard may be truthful (to the extent that they describe what is of the order of natural agreement) but shortsighted (to the extent that a private system is taken to "have more of the image of the universal").[80]

Edwards offers a uniquely integrated scheme of moral philosophy, one that expresses the idea that the moral life is nothing less than participation in the divine life. Whereas other approaches to virtue ethics lack an ontological scheme and essentially follow Aristotle to a private or limited domain, Edwards moves beyond such limited reflection and offers a dynamic conception of the moral life. In so doing, he contributes a theological construct that can be enormously useful for reflection upon the moral life.

For this reason, understanding Edwards's concept of consent is critical. As he puts it, true virtue "consists in a disposition to benevolence towards being in general."[81] He uses the language of "disposition" to benevolence. Delattre interprets this as a significant nuance in his theory of virtue: "Settled dispositions or habits or patterns of activity, not momentary visions or occasional acts, are what count. And the truly virtuous disposition or habit or pattern is primarily one of consent or benevolence to 'being simply considered.'"[82]

78. Ibid., 68.
79. Ibid., 87.
80. Ibid., 88.
81. Ibid., 5.
82. Ibid.

USES OF EDWARDS'S MORAL SCHEME IN THEOLOGY TODAY

I move now to consider Edwards's idea of virtue in light of the features of virtue ethics delineated earlier in this chapter. How might his understanding of virtue add to the current discussions on the theme of virtue in theological ethics and contribute to a construct of virtue for pastoral theology? How might his ideas of being, beauty, and consent contribute to modern discussions of virtue?

Aesthetic Theology as an Integrative Approach

I noted earlier that the complexities of forming a dialogue with the disciplines of moral philosophy, theological ethics, and pastoral theology provide a formidable task. What Edwards's approach to the topic especially offers toward such dialogue is a theological framework broad enough to manage these complexities. The aesthetic category of beauty he articulates offers a fresh approach to thinking about virtue.

Edwards cites this as a clear starting point for discussions about ethics and the moral life in his opening paragraph of *True Virtue*: "Whatever controversies and variety of opinions there are about the nature of virtue, yet all excepting some sceptics, who deny any real difference between virtue and vice, mean by it something beautiful, or rather some kind of beauty or excellency."[83] By offering the aesthetic concept of *beauty* as the framework from which the moral life is construed, he moves away from traditional religious argumentation. He does not argue for a Christian version of Aristotelian ethics (as Aquinas does), nor does he comment on the traditional split between the "moral virtues" and the "theological virtues." Instead he moves beyond these dichotomies, viewing the moral life as part of a "relational ontology."

Consent is as much an aesthetic category in Edwards as it is a moral concept. It involves more than the will. It involves dispositions or habits, what he terms the "sense of the heart." In Edwardsean psychology, the mind, heart, and will form a unity. By offering an aesthetic theology, he moves beyond the boundaries of traditional theological language. This is not to avoid discussions in Christian theology concerning the moral life, but to go beyond these by offering a conceptual framework that includes the ideas of sanctification, holiness, redemption, etc. His aesthetic

---

83. Edwards, *True Virtue*, 1.

theology has the capacity to envision the moral life in a dynamic, relational ontology. By defining virtue as "consent to being," he locates moral activity at the center of humanity's relationship to God and to one another. Love for God and love for one's neighbor, common themes in theological ethics, are not dealt with as separate moral functions but as part of an entire dynamic relational vision of the moral life.

Beauty then replaces duty as the gauge of the moral life. Virtuous actions are not assessed on the weight of their moral contribution or correctness but on the basis of their agreement or consent with God. There is an intimate link between God's infinite self-repetition of love and the development of moral character in the lives of those who are being transformed by grace.

Delattre takes Edwards's concept of beauty to be one of the most impressive features of his treatise on true virtue. He writes, "Beauty provides Edwards with a model of the structure and dynamics of the moral life and of its proper objective foundation, which yet makes the categories of vision and perception, of imagination and discernment, fundamental to the moral and religious life."[84] Through his concept of beauty, Edwards elevates his thought concerning virtue beyond discussions of moral imperatives and deontological sequences, locating the moral life within the structure of being itself.

The modern situation requires Christian theologians to speak relevantly to an increasingly complex world situation. With the widening scope of understanding concerning the various cultures, languages, and worldviews in theology today, Edwards's moral scheme offers an important alternative to the ways we structure our reflection on the theme of virtue.[85]

---

84. Delattre, *Beauty and Sensibility*, 113.

85. Delattre writes: "It is my view that by attending to the critical importance of beauty in Edwards' vision of reality we are not only able to discern more accurately what he thought; we are also able to appreciate more fully precisely those dimensions of his intellectual achievement which hold the greatest promise of relevance to theological and moral reflection in our time ... Edwards' thought gives promise of shedding important light when approached in terms of its aesthetic dimensions, particularly where the issues involve the development of models for the structure and dynamics of the moral life." Delattre, "Beauty and Theology," 148.

Religious Experience and the Moral Life

While many would begin their search for moral foundations in rational philosophy, I would argue that Edwards's own experience of conversion became a paradigm for authentic theological searching throughout his life. He did not de-emphasize the importance of religious experience but rather sought ways to reflect on those experiences in the light of Scripture and the debates in theology relevant to his day. His attempts to understand his own religious conversion and the experiences of others in the revivals in his own congregation and throughout New England are an important part of his theological reflections and writings.[86] In the end, he was able to articulate a vision for the moral life that took seriously the religious experiences he had encountered (both his own and those of the revivals), and incorporated these into the wider aesthetic conception of God's activity in the world.

His search for understanding of the experiences of the heart reflect more a personal quest than a scientific inquiry. In *The Nature of True Virtue* he composed a final treatise on his understanding of the moral life. Here he went far beyond his analysis of religious experience in *Religious Affections* and formulated a theological framework for conceiving the moral life in all of its aspects, including religious awakenings and sense perceptions.

Earlier I described one of the important features of a virtue ethic as being able to express the subtle nuances of moral participation. Edwards's own system of thought uses language that is experience-sensitive. Subtleties that he addresses include impressions on the mind, sensations, affections of the heart, consent/agreement/dissent, attitudes, and so on. The moral life is not to be understood as a compilation of moral quandaries to be decided about or a series of consequential choices. Instead, he understands the moral life in terms of a spiritual or moral apprehension. The functions of the moral life are defined by our ability to perceive the activity of God (by grace) and to agree or offer heartfelt consent. His complex analysis of the moral life predates the attempts of modern pastoral theology to understand religious convictions and their relationship to the moral life. By examining these subtle features of the moral formation of the believer, he offers a constructive theological framework for pastoral theology and virtue theory.

---

86. For an excellent analysis of Edwards's conceptions of religious experience, see Proudfoot, "From Theology to a Science of Religions."

Social Dimensions of Virtue

Edwards insists that true virtue attends not only to a localized or "private sphere" but also to the wider connections in which virtuous actions consent with being in general. In proposing this idea of the moral life, he offers a theological account useful for modern theories of ethics that emphasize a comprehensive context for the functions of the moral life. Moral vision, in his scheme, requires the agent of moral action to perceive such action "comprehensively" and "universally," "with regard to all its tendencies, and its connections with everything to which it stands related."[87] Virtue cannot be contained in the character of individuals outside of their broader social context. It is rather in the broader association with all of its connections, ultimately its connection with the Divine life, that virtue must be understood. In his descriptions of consent to being, Edwards understands the social complexion of the moral life as a multiplicity of relations. These relations, as Delattre points out, are "primarily objective, structural, relational, and creative or formative, rather than primarily subjective, emotional, relativist, and created or well-formed."[88] Virtue is always to be understood in its wider context.

For Edwards, this ultimately led to an ontological framework that expressed an understanding of the moral life in relation to God's own activity in time and space. However, the significance of his scheme for moral relationship at lesser levels must not be overlooked. It is here that he contributes an understanding of the moral life that is able to include both the moral vision of the believer and the unbeliever. The defining character of true virtue is not in some spiritual interiority but rather in one's ability to see the wider relations of their moral actions. In the end, he conceives this ability to be related to one's love for God, that is, to the extent that a person is able to understand her moral actions as relating to God as the "being of beings." Nonetheless, the various dimensions of a social ethic can be observed in Edwards's relational and aesthetic theology.

The moral life must be understood, therefore, from the perspective not of private virtues being lived out in isolation, but of our interconnectedness and, in particular, with our relation to God as the infinite Being. There is, in his system, an inversion of the usual approach to social

---

87. Edwards, *True Virtue*, 3.
88. Delattre, "Beauty and Theology," 140.

ethics in theology. Rather than beginning with love for God and neighbor and construing moral precepts and understandings, we discover in Edwards a system of moral participation in which our widening scope of virtuous activity will result in more love to neighbor and, ultimately to God. Moral vision is therefore not the result of increasing obedience or moral regimen but rather of increasing awareness of the connectedness of our moral acts in relation to being in general.

CONCLUSION

Virtue ethics is a growing area of study in modern moral philosophy. I have argued that Edwards's concept of virtue is a useful concept for the formulation of a specifically theological vision of virtue. His moral scheme includes all of the common dimensions of virtue ethics: it is teleological in character, it conveys an understanding of human agency in the moral life, it describes the subtle nuances of the moral life, it offers a dynamic interpretation of the universal connection of virtues with each other, and it comprehends the moral life from the wider framework of the community and beyond. Beyond this, it is a scheme of moral philosophy that includes a biblical vision of God's character as expressed in the universe and connected with our moral actions through the vehicle of consent. It is this final leap toward the Infinite that moves us beyond the difficulties of combining fields as wide in scope as pastoral theology, theological ethics, and moral philosophy/theology. Moral formation and moral action consist of "benevolence to being in general,"[89] or, "to speak more accurately, it is that consent, propensity and union of heart to being in general, which is immediately exercised in a general good will."[90]

---

89. Edwards, *True Virtue*, 3.
90. Ibid.

3

The Language of Moral Vision

INTRODUCTION

MY INTENTION HERE IS to build on the foundation of Edwards's ontological scheme of virtue outlined in the previous chapter by introducing the theme of suffering as an integrative motif from the perspective of pastoral theology. I will argue that reflection on the nature of true virtue from the vantage point of pastoral theology demands more than an understanding of "consent to being" as delineated by Edwards. Specifically, I advance the proposal that attention to suffering, which is integral to the discipline of pastoral theology, modifies and strengthens Edwards's relational ontology of virtue.

Edwards's own framework and conceptualization of virtue lends itself to such a proposal. By arguing for the relationship between all things as "consent to being," his ontological framework implies also a structural ontology of suffering. That is to say, if our experiences of beauty have a structural relation to each other, the same thing must be said of our experiences of suffering. Following Edwards's idea of consent, suffering must ultimately have its essential structure in the experience of suffering being to suffering being. If God is the supreme being, then the nature of suffering must have its ontological reference point in God's own suffering. Though it goes beyond the scope of this work to expound the nature of God's suffering, this effort to introduce suffering into the fabric of virtue theory itself may be seen as a parallel effort to those recent approaches in theology that attempt to develop the concept of a suffering God. While few would today debate the importance of understanding God as One who suffers with us, in *The Creative Suffering of God* Paul Fiddes suggests that "careful examination is needed of what it means to talk about the suffering of God."[1] He is concerned that while many are happy to speak of a God who suffers, few are prepared to face up to the full implications of such a theological stance. While they are prepared to "invoke the theme of a suffering God," there is a reluctance to "follow it through into a theology that embraces divine weakness at the centre," thereby diffusing it of "its explosive effect upon the whole doctrine of God."[2]

Conceptually, the idea of virtue as a pastoral theological construct connects the sense of suffering with another to God's own pathos or suffering. This demands a particular use of language and an attentiveness to what I call here the language of moral vision. I will argue that in the connections of suffering being with suffering being, there is a unique perspective on the nature of virtue that transcends Edwards's concept of "consent to being."

Before turning to a constructive proposal in the next chapter, I offer here a description of the ways that we can begin to speak meaningfully about the integration of the experiences or encounters with suffering and the language of moral vision. This chapter will explore how the experience of suffering provides the occasion for moral insight. In my view, the moral life needs to be conceived from a framework that includes all dimensions of experience, including our encounters with suffering. This argument involves three steps.

First, I address the question of language and the meanings that we attach to the suffering moments in our life. I follow those in the field of pastoral theology who have suggested that poetry may be a useful way of voicing critical experiences of suffering if it follows the transforming word-form of parable. My own contribution to this discussion is to suggest that the moral dimensions of the suffering moment may come to light by reframing our experience as moral insight.

Second, I explain the sense of personal history in which one might experience one's life as a journey or quest toward the integration of experiences of suffering as a way of conceiving the life of moral development. I contend that those who are particularly engaged in pastoral care need to learn to reflect on their own journey of suffering and to connect those experiences with a moral vision for the good. Autobiographical accounts are explored in this regard.

---

1. Fiddes, *Creative Suffering*, 1.
2. Ibid.

Third, I follow this discussion of the quest with a section on moral vision itself. I employ S. Dennis Ford's argument that one of the important tasks of moral vision is debunking myths that reinforce indifference.³ I argue further that in the enterprise of pastoral care our responsibility moves beyond debunking to offer constructive proposals about how to live. In this respect moral vision needs to move toward the articulate expression of the life of virtue itself.

LANGUAGE AND THE EXPERIENCE OF SUFFERING

According to Simone Weil, the function of language "is to express the relationship between things."⁴ In this section, I will explore the use of language in expressing the relationship between suffering and virtue. If we are to speak meaningfully of experiences of suffering, we need to pay careful attention to how language may express the depths of these experiences. We must find ways to express the experiences of suffering in order that its deeper dimensions are enabled to find their way out. We need to look for those word-forms that capture and express the ultimate anxieties and the sublime hopes that wrestle for supremacy in our hearts.

Language and the Depth Dimension of Reality

In *Theology of Culture*, Paul Tillich examines the role of language in religious thought. According to him, words can function either as "signs" or as "symbols." Both signs and symbols "point beyond themselves to something else."⁵ The difference is that while symbols participate in the reality to which they point, signs do not. The moment a word acquires a connotation that moves beyond its function as a pointing sign, it becomes a symbol. Tillich observes that we use words both as signs and as symbols. When used as symbols, as in liturgical or poetic language,⁶ words open up a hidden level of reality, or "the depth dimension of reality."⁷ Such powerful symbols have a corresponding "interior reality"⁸ in the soul.

---

3. Ford, *Sins of Omission*.
4. Weil, *Gravity and Grace*, 3.
5. Tillich, *Theology of Culture*, 54.
6. Ibid., 56.
7. Ibid., 59.
8. Ibid., 57.

Thus, poetic language functions as a bridge between the interior experience of a soul and the exterior or depth dimension of reality. As he says, "Religious symbols open up the experience of the dimension of this depth in the human soul."[9]

This analysis is helpful for a pastoral theology that seeks to understand the connection of virtue and suffering. At the symbolic level, where words point to meanings beyond themselves, one begins to form a way of speaking about the unspeakable. Poetic language can thus be seen as a way of expressing a deeper reality. In Tillich's own view, the connection between the depth dimension of reality (ontology) and the interior reality of the soul (experience) finds expression through the artistry of poetic word-forms.[10]

Tillich's concept of religious language as symbol provides one important connection between suffering and virtue. It offers a basis for connecting Edwards's relational ontology of virtue with religious symbols expressing the experiences of suffering. If poetic language expresses the level of the soul (interior reality) with the corresponding hidden dimension of being itself (the depth dimension), this offers an important way of speaking about virtue and suffering together.

Such speaking is familiar to the language of the Bible. The effort to express ultimate reality through symbol-bearing language is a common feature of the Scriptures. Commenting on the relationship between the search for ultimate expression of reality and the language of the Bible, Tillich concludes:

> Some of the greatest of those who have searched for ultimate reality spoke in a way that is very similar to the way in which the Bible speaks. The term "blindness" for the ordinary state of mind is used in all periods of philosophical thought. The experience of being awakened out of the sleep of the natural worldview, the sudden awareness of the light of the ontological question, the breaking-through the surface on which one lived and moved before—these events are described like a religious conversion . . . Ontology presupposes a conversion, an opening of the eyes, a

---

9. Ibid., 59.

10. Ibid., 56–57. Here, Tillich expresses the view that art opens different levels of reality and that there is a significant difference in function between philosophical language and poetic language.

revelatory experience. It is not a matter of detached observation, analysis, and hypothesis.[11]

Of particular significance is his insistence on the proximity of ontology and "an opening of the eyes" as a basis for speaking of ultimate reality. Much of our language seems to have the effect of lulling us to sleep, of "closing" our eyes. Detached observation, calculating analysis, and dry hypotheses fail to break through. What is needed are word-forms (symbols) that participate in that to which they point, word-forms that express the depth dimension of reality and open up the soul.[12]

In order to offer such meaningful expression one must be immersed in ultimate reality. Tillich insists that only those who are "involved in ultimate reality," who have "encountered it as a matter of existential concern, can try to speak about it meaningfully."[13] I would argue that pastors are uniquely postured for such expression. Among the primary concerns of the pastor is the caring action of moving into the sacred experiences of suffering with others.

Tillich's distinction between "symbol" and "sign" provides an important distinction in the use of language to describe the depth dimension of reality. Unlike the sign, the symbol participates in the reality to which it points. The use of symbolic language provides the necessary connection between Edwards's relational ontology and idea of virtue and the experience of suffering. In order to speak meaningfully about the depth dimension, an "opening of the eyes" is required. The metaphorical use of the term "blindness" indicates an inability to see or to express a moral vision that is consonant with the depth dimension. The pastor, as a participant in matters of ultimate concern, is postured uniquely not only to "see" but also to express what is "seen" through the symbols of the depth dimension. To speak of the very depths of suffering is therefore an inherently virtuous act, and is at the heart of the pastoral participation in the depth dimension of ultimate reality.

Breaking the Silence of Suffering

The experiences of suffering are not easily articulated. Many who suffer in silence long for an understanding person to assist in the reflection

11. Tillich, *Biblical Religion*, 65.
12. Tillich, *Theology of Culture*, 57.
13. Tillich, *Biblical Religion*, 65.

necessary to word the Void and to give meaning to the suffering through the use of language. Precisely by entering into the pain-filled quest that such suffering brings, the pastor is in a position to attempt this articulation through language. This is what Henry Nouwen describes as "sensitive articulation."[14] If the expression of suffering articulated is to be helpful, however, the pastor will need to identify her own encounters with suffering as a participation in the existential anxiety of the broken world. That is to say, the sensitive articulation of suffering necessarily includes one's own suffering. As a sojourner in the community of the afflicted, the pastor is not only one who listens and articulates the suffering of others, but is also a co-participant in the brokenness of the world. Vulnerability is therefore an important factor in the articulation of suffering.

In this respect, Nouwen issues a plea in *The Wounded Healer* that we make our wounds available as a source of healing for others. He contends that ministry will not be perceived as authentic unless it comes from a heart that has itself been wounded by the suffering of which it speaks. Pastoral care requires a two-fold attention to the suffering of others encountered in the pastoral interaction and to the suffering in one's own heart. Only in this way will "sensitive articulation" be possible. Articulation of the depths of the wounded soul requires self-conscious solidarity with those who suffer. As Nouwen states: "Making one's wounds a source of healing, therefore, does not call for a sharing of superficial pains but for a constant willingness to see one's own pain and suffering as rising from the depth of the human condition which all [persons] share."[15]

This dual articulation of one's own suffering and that of others is comparable to what Dorothy Soelle refers to as the movement from mutism to lament.[16] She insists that the story of suffering must be told if there are to be any meaningful actions against suffering. Mutism is the experience of the suffering. That is, those suffering are unable to express the unspeakable pain in which they are immersed. But the experience of suffering needs to find expression if it is to be overcome: "The first step . . . is, then, to find a language that leads out of the uncomprehended suffering that makes one mute, a language of lament, of crying, or pain,

---

14. Nouwen, *Wounded Healer*, 39.
15. Ibid., 88.
16. Soelle, *Suffering*, 70.

a language that at least says what the situation is."[17] This breaking of the silence of suffering requires a word-form appropriate to the task. Soelle suggests the use of the lament as a subversive prayer-form. The prayer of lament, says Soelle, "is an act by which people dare to put their desires into words and thereby handle their suffering differently from the way society recommends to them."[18]

The aim of lament for Soelle is not a full theological explanation of the suffering moment. In fact, she is critical of theologians for their "intolerable passion for explaining and speaking when silence would be appropriate."[19] Thus, the lament is more experience-near than are the explanations and scientific language of theology. The aim of the lament is simply "to at least say what the situation is." Description and authentic expression are the aims of the prayer of lament.

The prayer of lament is a word-form appropriate to the anguish— the depth dimension—of suffering. Soelle suggests that the literary genre of the lament psalms speak meaningfully to the three dimensions of suffering: its physical, psychological, and social dimensions.[20] In her view, "suffering as it appears in the lament threatens every dimension of life."[21]

Breaking the silence is an important function of language in the work of pastoral care. To take seriously one's own suffering as a participant in the brokenness of the world involves critical self-reflection. But more than this, breaking the silence requires a sensitive articulation that gives meaningful expression to all the dimensions of suffering, including physical pain, psychological numbness, and social degradation. The prayer-form of lament is a most appropriate form of language for moving from the situation of mutism to articulation of the experience of suffering in its dimensional depths. The lament is not an attempt to explain or rationalize but rather is an experience-near word-form that breaks the immobilizing power of the experience of suffering by articulating its depths. It is a cry for help.

17. Ibid.
18. Ibid., 78.
19. Ibid., 19.
20. Ibid., 16.
21. Ibid.

Poetry and Theology

As a way of illuminating through the forming of words, poetry is a most useful way of addressing the complexities of suffering and virtue. Poetry has been variously described as a work of art sprung from necessity, an infinite loneliness,[22] and an undesired pregnancy.[23] As Rilke advises the young, aspiring poet:

> Everything is gestation and then bringing forth. To let each impression and each germ of feeling come to completion wholly in itself, in the dark, in the inexpressible, the unconscious, beyond the reach of one's own intelligence, and await with deep humility and patience the birth hour of a new clarity . . .[24]

Walter Brueggemann also identifies the poetic word as a corrective, especially in the ministry of proclamation:

> To address the issue of a truth greatly reduced requires us to be poets that speak against a prose world. The terms of that phrase are readily misunderstood. By prose I refer to a world that is organized in settled formulae, so that even pastoral prayers and love letters sound like memos. By poetry, I do not mean rhyme, rhythm, or meter, but language that moves . . . that jumps at the right moment, that breaks open old worlds with surprise, abrasion, and pace . . . The tensive interface between a reduced world of prose and a poetic speech of vitality requires us to consider the peculiar role of dramatic, poetic communication, the very kind given us in the text of the Bible.[25]

The Brazilian theologian/philosopher Rubem Alves also advocates poetry as a particular form of theological expression in *The Poet, the Prophet, the Warrior*. He notes, "Poets are among the few who perceive the farce. They show that the king is naked."[26] Through the poetic way of speaking, we soon recognize that our ability to control the words is in-

---

22. Rilke, *Letters to a Young Poet*. Rilke speaks of the authentic work of poetry as something that "has sprung from necessity" and that is experienced as "an infinite loneliness." Ibid., 20.

23. Alves, *Poet, Prophet, Warrior*, 67. Alves speaks of the creative act as "an undesired pregnancy." He continues, "Creativity . . . is a forbidden act, therefore, the creative act takes place almost totally underground."

24. Rilke, *Letters to a Young Poet*, 29.

25. Brueggemann, *Finally Comes the Poet*, 3–4.

26. Alves, *Poet, Warrior, Prophet*, 112.

adequate. Poetry moves us to the place where the words exert their own will. It initiates movement back to "the founding Word, which emerges out of silence."[27] It is the place of accepting that the words have their own will: "Every word is filled with f/lights beyond our control. In prose we have the word: birds in cages. In poetry the words explode the cage in which they were trapped, and they fly and take us on their wings."[28]

Words released from the obligation of the pen find their own flight and present ways of seeing that spring from the pregnant reality of God's first Word. As Alves notes, poetry begins when we place ourselves before the Void to wait in silence for the Word:

> "Creation ex nihilo"—out of nothing. There are words which grow out of ten thousand things and words which grow out of other words: endless . . . But there is a Word which emerges out of silence, the Word which is the beginning of the world. This Word cannot be produced. It is neither a child of our hands or of our thoughts. We have to wait in silence, till it makes itself heard: Advent . . . Grace.[29]

The poem, then, may be seen as a subversive word-form that breaks out of the prison/cage of prose. When challenged by the expert in hermeneutics to explain what he meant to say, the poet replies:

> I wanted to say precisely what I said. There is no way of improving a poem. None of its words can be exchanged by a synonym. As with the cathedral, its darkness cannot be exchanged for light, its silence for words. "What I said is precisely what I wanted to say because this is what I saw," says the poet.[30]

Alves's contrast between the poetic word and the word of prose[31] may be summarized via the following table:

---

27. Ibid., 4.
28. Ibid., 102.
29. Ibid., 3.
30. Ibid., 101.
31. Ibid., 100.

Poetry	Prose
One single word pregnant with unpredictable meanings	Many words to say one simple, solid and stable meaning
One word that leads to infinite horizons	Many words that are a funnel that leads to one single, precise meaning
In poetry one does not know what one is talking about	In prose one knows what one is talking about
Poetry is being, not doing	Prose is knowledge
Words have their own will	Words are trapped in cages

Essential to Alves's view is that words should not be domesticated. He points to the Reformation as a time where the Word was released:

> Every individual was to read the scriptures as one reads a poem, alone, without any intervening voices of interpretation. Hermenuets were to be silent, so that the believer could hear the voice of the Stranger: the inner testimony of the Holy Spirit . . . If, by sheer grace, the Wind blew and the melody which was not there was heard, the dead would be resurrected.[32]

The power of the poetic word-form, then, promises to break through in ways that other word-forms will fail. The poem has the potential to release words in such a way as to let the reader be confronted by the first Word.

The Parabolic Nature of Poetry

Donald Capps has long been concerned with the matter of language in pastoral theology. Of particular importance is his emphasis on the relationship between the similarities of texts and pastoral actions. In *Pastoral Care and Hermeneutics* he follows Paul Ricoeur in understanding texts as "world-disclosing."[33] The relationship of the reader and the text is thus seen to be one of "reciprocal interpretation." Although we interpret texts, texts also interpret us. This view of "reciprocal interpretation"[34] has particular relevance to the form of biblical text known as the parable. The parable has a unique world-disclosing power due to its

---

32. Ibid., 102.
33. Capps, *Pastoral Care and Hermeneutics*, 19.
34. Ibid., 20.

The Language of Moral Vision

capacity to reorient us through a pattern of "orientation, disorientation, and reorientation."[35] In this view, the parable radically reorients us to the world.

In *The Poet's Gift*, Capps puts forward the provocative proposal that poetry may be seen as a source of renewal for pastoral care. In his discussion of language, he identifies the parallels between the modern-day poem and the ancient parable of the Bible, noting five key similarities:[36]

(a) Brevity. "Like the parable, the poem is typically much briefer and more compressed than the novel or the short story."[37] The poem's brief encounter with a specific life situation allows it to penetrate the various dimensions of a particular experience without attempting to locate it within a larger conceptual framework. This allows the experience to be articulated in ways that reflect the unique dimensions of reality without the constraint of attempting to explain it in a broader theological scheme.

(b) Episodic character. "Like the parable . . . the poem is episodic, usually concerned with a single life event or experience, with little or no attempt to explain how this event or experience fits within the larger life structure of the poet or the poet's subject."[38] By episodic I do not mean that the experience has no continuity within a life structure. Rather, the interpretation of the experience focuses on the experience in all its particularity, even, at times, seeming triviality. Experience stands alone without the need for its incorporation into a larger from of meaning or significance.

(c) Extended Metaphor. "Like the parable, the poem is an extended metaphor, the meaning of which is expressed by the poem itself . . . one does not look outside the poem for the 'point' of the poem, since the poem is the point."[39] Poems have a self-contained meaning. They express a dimension or understanding of the situation that calls for attentive listening rather than

---

35. Ibid., 28.
36. Capps, *Poet's Gift*.
37. Ibid., 2.
38. Ibid.
39. Ibid.

analysis. The extended metaphor stands for itself and speaks for itself. It requires no further interpretation.

(d) Open-endedness. "Like the parable, the poem is necessarily open-ended. Its goal is not to tell a complete story, as a novel does, but to use a life episode—often one that is seemingly unimportant or that other, less perceptive eyes would have overlooked—to inspire or even prod the reader to look at life in a different way."[40] Poetry has a capacity to bring about a certain kind of reflection. It does not bring the dialogue to a conclusion, but prompts, interrupts, and prods in a particular way. Perhaps it is this feature of poetry that enables it to move from sign to symbol, provoking deeper insight into what may seem unimportant episodes.

(e) Unorthodoxy/Radicality. "Like Jesus' parables, poems are usually considered unorthodox, if not radical, precisely because they challenge our usual and routine ways of perceiving and construing our life experiences, enticing us into viewing them from a different angle or slant."[41] The poem, then, may be understood as a brief, episodic, open-ended, and often radical extended metaphor. Its purpose, like the parable, is to transform our worldview and to offer a fresh perspective on the life situation.

Reframing or Re-forming?

In a related work on the use of parable in pastoral care, Capps recommends the method of "reframing" as a new method for pastoral care in specific situations.[42] As defined by its originators, reframing "means to change the conceptual and/or emotional setting or viewpoint in relation to which a situation is experienced and to place it in another frame which fits the 'facts' of the same concrete situation equally well or better, and thereby changes its meaning."[43] Capps suggests that Jesus' own parables had this reframing goal in mind. Jesus wanted to bring a new perspective to bear on a situation and often used parables for this purpose. The aim of reframing is to allow persons to see their situation from a new

40. Ibid.
41. Ibid.
42. Capps, *Reframing*.
43. Watzlawick, Weakland, and Fisch, *Change*, 95.

angle and to approach their problems from a completely new orientation. Capps suggests that the tool of reframing is a potentially valuable method in pastoral care and counseling.

In my view, reframing may touch an even deeper dimension of the person, allowing for a change of moral posture. In this respect, the parable/poem may not only reorient the person to their situation but may also change their stance in the situation. If so, I suggest the term "re-forming" as it pertains to the character, disposition, and the affections of the person as a moral agent. As Watzlawick et al. point out: "Reframing operates on the level of *meta*reality, where . . . change can take place even if the objective circumstances of a situation are quite beyond human control." This metareality level may correspond to what Tillich has termed "the depth dimension."[44] The parable form (or modern poem) may be useful, then, not only as a linguistic tool to reframe a situation but also as a source of moral insight, a re-forming that concerns moral vision and character. Applied to situations of extreme suffering, the reframing method may be understood as touching the moral dimension as a re-forming. This reformation not only seeks to "sensitively articulate" the situation—its depth dimensions—but also offers a new orientation to the situation resulting in moral insight and a fundamental change of moral posture in the world. In this way, the poem may in fact go far beyond challenging our perceptions and viewpoint of the world. If Jesus' own articulation of the realities of the reign of God were succinctly stated in the transforming parable, then perhaps, in much the same way, the parable/poem is truly re-formational.

Thus, the poem's task is not only to "open our eyes," but also radically to alter our moral posture in the world, to undo our prefabricated answers to life's ultimate questions, and to re-form our character. Like poetic speaking, parabolic speaking questions us. It interprets us. It declares our need for grace to change us. The parable is not a hint or a clue but a radical challenge. It is not meant to shape, but to reshape, to change us from within. In this sense, its purpose is nothing less than moral conversion.

Such was Jesus' use of parables in the Gospels. They were intended to undo power. They were subversive word-forms meant to explode the cages of the Pharisees' fabricated religion and stale dogma. They were, in

---

44. Ibid., 97.

fact, intended to reveal "the hidden things." Hence Matthew's explanation for Jesus' use of parables:

> All these things Jesus spoke to the multitudes in parables, and He did not speak to them without a parable, so that what was spoken through the prophet might be fulfilled, saying, "I will open my mouth in parables; I will utter things hidden since the foundation of the world." (Matt 13:34–35; NASB)

In short, I am arguing that poetic language is the form of discourse that enables us to give expression to the complex confluence of suffering and virtue. Poetic language has the capacity to re-form the character or disposition of a person, to change a person from indifferent observer of suffering, to concerned but mute empathic participant in suffering, to one who is able to give voice to the experience of suffering in the depths of all its dimensions (physical, psychological, and social). This reformation takes us to the "hidden things" and ruptures answers (to questions) through the risk of daring, graceful vulnerability.

PASTORAL THEOLOGY AS QUEST FOR MORAL VISION

Early pioneers in the field of pastoral theology such as Anton Boisen viewed their task as giving comfort, hope, courage, and peace of mind to the suffering. Their passion for pastoral care was rooted in a fundamental dream for the general good of others. In particular, it represented a vision of suffering with others. As previously noted, Boisen expressed his dream in this way: "I am hoping and laboring for the day when the specialist in religion will be able with his help to go down to the depths of the grim abyss after those who are capable of responding, those in whom some better self is seeking to come to birth."[45] Boisen here identifies the concern of the field of pastoral theology as fundamentally a particular kind of participation in the suffering of others. Care and involvement are at the center of the enterprise. Therefore, one way to view the aim of pastoral theology as a whole is to think of it as a quest to bring hope into the grim abyss of personal and communal suffering. I turn now to consider the quest for moral vision as the particular expression of solidarity with those who suffer.

---

45. Boisen, "Distinctive Task," 12.

The word "quest" goes beyond the familiar use of "questions,"[46] which come up in investigations that are primarily rational. "Quest" involves the mind, heart, and will, and implies that one is embarking on a journey. Such questing is at the heart of the pastoral theological enterprise, which concerns itself with the articulation of the depth dimension of the experience of suffering and with the capacity of hope to redeem suffering. A quest may be seen as having four characteristics.

A Quest Demands Pursuit

Unlike other enterprises that are chosen from among many possibilities, the quest chooses the person. The quest unfolds as consent to the particular experiences that shape one's life. It thus involves consent to a destiny that is not necessarily of one's own choosing. In his autobiography, Jurgen Moltmann remembers the manner in which the quest for framing his experiences theologically became his own. He describes himself as one of the generation "which consciously lived through the horrors of the Second World War, the collapse of an empire and all its institutions, the guilt and shame of one's own nation, and a long period as prisoner of war."[47] Witnessing these horrors demanded a response. Coming out of the camps and hospitals as survivors meant never seeing the world in quite the same way. The surviving experienced themselves as "burnt children who from then on shunned the fire."[48]

Despite the sombre burden of guilt and the inconsolable grief that comes with such experiences, he speaks of a compulsion to "create a new, different, more humane world. Some of us found behind the barbed wire the power of a hope which wants something new."[49] As a result of his experience as a prisoner of war (from February 1945 to April 1948) Moltmann gave up his dream of studying mathematics and physics. He describes the anguish of coming to terms with the revelation of the crimes committed in Germany's name—Buchenwald, Auschwitz, Maidanak, Bergen-Belsen—while sitting in his prison cell in Belgium:

> And with that came the necessity of standing up to it all inwardly, shut up in camps as we were. I think my own little world fell to

---

46. I owe the distinction here to Kreeft, *Making Sense out of Suffering*, 24.
47. Moltmann, *Experiences of God*, 6.
48. Ibid.
49. Ibid.

pieces then too . . . In that Belgian camp, hungry as we were, I saw how other men collapsed inwardly, how they gave up hope, sickening for the lack of it, some of them dying. The same thing almost happened to me.[50]

He chooses words carefully: "the necessity of standing up to it all;" "they gave up all hope;" "the same thing almost happened to me." The quest is inspired by the seriousness of the reality confronted. Seeing his fellow prisoners sickening and dying for lack of hope, a response from the aspiring physicist was required, one that he refers to as "an experience of God."

> It was the experience of God's presence in the dark night of the soul: "If I make my bed in hell, behold, thou art there." A well-meaning army chaplain had given me a New Testament. I thought it was out of place. I would rather have had something to eat. But then I became fascinated by the Psalms (which were printed as an appendix) and especially by Psalm 39: "I was dumb with silence, I held my peace, even from good; and my sorrow was stirred" (but the German is much stronger—"I have to eat up my grief within myself!") . . . "Hold thou not thy peace at my tears: for I am a stranger with thee, and a sojourner, as all my fathers were." These psalms gave me the words for my own suffering. They opened my eyes to the God who is with those "that are of a broken heart." He was present even behind the barbed wire—no, most of all behind the barbed wire.[51]

Words fed the quest. They came as words of life. While bread would have been more desirable, the naive army chaplain had given words—hopeful words, transforming words, words of God's presence in the midst of the soul's dark night.

Thirty years later Moltmann articulates what happened to him in that prison camp:

> Perhaps there are certain deeply rooted experiences in every life which mould existence and sustain it at the same time. We return to them again and again, recalling them and thinking them over. We continually give them a new interpretation. As we enter into them they become present, and the time that cuts us off from them ceases to exist . . . That is the way I still experience today what I went through over thirty years ago. It was those

---

50. Ibid., 7.
51. Ibid., 7, 8.

experiences that induced me to give up my dream of mathematics and physics, Einstein and Planck, and study theology.[52]

Moltmann came to see his life in terms of a "sojourn" or "pilgrimage." Hope was reborn. He comes to speak of an encounter with God as a comforting presence in the face of "affliction" or "the dark night of the soul." He describes how he learned to watch his fellow prisoners become ill and die for lack of hope. His experience may be seen as "a transforming moment."[53] The prisoner of hope was eventually to become the theologian of hope. Such is the nature of the convictional experience. It compels one to move in a direction that resonates with the depth of one's experiences. The "experience of God" in "the dark night of the soul," where hope was diminished and almost extinguished, is not the end of the quest, but its beginning. It awakens and invigorates the ensuing pursuit.

A Quest Pushes toward the Boundaries

In *The Courage to Be*, Paul Tillich asserts that courage is self-affirmation "in spite of" the triple anxiety of death, meaninglessness, and guilt that together move one towards the boundary line of despair.[54] His insights into the ontological questions of faith and existence assist in further clarifying the meaning of a quest. According to Tillich, faith must be understood not as a theoretical affirmation of something uncertain, but rather, as "the existential acceptance of something transcending ordinary experience . . . It is the state of being grasped by the power of being which transcends everything that is and in which everything that is participates . . . faith is the basis of the courage to be."[55]

Such "absolute faith" is an important dimension of the quest. It has three critical elements. The first element is "the experience of *the power of being* which is present even in the face of the most radical manifestation of non-being."[56] In this experience of the power of being there is a sense in which "vitality resists despair,"[57] which, for Tillich, is intimately

---

52. Ibid., 9.
53. Loder, *Transforming Moment*.
54. Tillich, *Courage to Be*, 41.
55. Ibid., 169.
56. Ibid., 171 (emphasis mine).
57. Ibid.

linked to a person's intentionality. Intentional hope resists despair. Thus, the first element of faith involves the refusal to acquiesce to despair. The second element is the conviction that even experiences of non-being and meaninglessness are dependent on experiences of being and meaning, for "even in the state of despair one has enough being to make despair possible."[58] The third element is "the acceptance of being accepted." Here, "the courage to be is rooted in the God who appears when God has disappeared in the anxiety of doubt."[59]

For Tillich, the boundaries of faith are expanded to the point where doubt and meaninglessness are absorbed. Absolute faith "is the situation on the boundary of [humanity's] possibility."[60] What that boundary may be is never fully known to the person of faith. Its pursuit requires the absolute courage to be. Such courage is more common, I believe, among ministers who understand their work as the confrontation of their own suffering and the suffering of others as a moral responsibility. The experience of being entrusted with stories of trauma, anxiety, fear, and horror, together with one's own suffering, pushes one toward boundaries otherwise inaccessible. To be a minister entails the commitment to this courage. The moral vision that derives from this courage is an important element in this push toward the boundaries. Pastoral theology is not content merely to describe situations of anguish but to articulate them in a way that presents a moral vision of what might be, how life could be otherwise than it is.

For example, in *The Child's Song* Donald Capps exposes the religious abuse of children. The travesty of abuse legitimized by religion warranted such an exposé. Capps describes his intention for writing on such a theme: "My concern here is with the child who, for whatever reason, lost the ability to sing the song or recite the poem that he or she had prepared. I am concerned with an important non event—with what was supposed to happen ... but was preempted by another agenda."[61] He expresses the longing for a church in which the child may sing for the first time, a simple chorus without having "already felt the slashing cruelties of life."[62] This attempt to challenge the status quo is a part of the moral

58. Ibid., 171–72.
59. Ibid., 183.
60. Ibid., 182.
61. Capps, *Child's Song*, xvii.
62. Ibid., 172.

courage of pastoral theology. It resonates with Simone Weil's visionary statement, "We have to say like Ivan Karmazov that nothing can make up for a single tear from a child."[63] The pastoral theologian confronts the realities of evil, thereby risking loss of personal security and beckoning a new kind of solidarity, one reflecting an absolute faith.

Of course, the tides do not always turn easily in one's favor when one speaks prophetically about the experiences of suffering. Yet, the challenge of Christopher Levan spurs on those who would-be-faithful. In *God Hates Religion*, he contends that

> God hates those servants who sit on their hands or who hide behind a wall of pious rationalizations feigning helplessness while evil mounts. The chief problem with an institutional religion is that it is unwilling to risk its life to correct injustice and bind up the broken-hearted. When out of self-serving fear or well-intentioned indolence the faith community remains aloof from the crises of this world that God loves, God is angered and dismayed.[64]

False boundaries are often delineated in terms that keep the fainthearted pastor from moral action. This is why a quest is preferable to a vocation. Vocations can be modified, adjusted, or even changed. The quest is non-negotiable. It chooses. It pushes toward the boundary, manifesting a faith that is ever-prepared to risk, even court, suffering.

A Quest is Imaginative

When a child pretends she is on an adventure, there is a sense of openness to the world, a feeling of great risk, and impending danger. There are battles to be fought that require strategic planning. Huge problems must be overcome to maintain safety and success. Rigorous demands are placed on the body, mind, and spirit. Playful imagination rallies all available resources. Real life is much the same. Pastoral intervention, much like the child's imaginative use of resources, requires imagination. Besides courage, the problems encountered require wisdom, faith, and love. Strategy is called for. Dangers lurk nearby. Risk is always a factor. The stakes are high. People's souls are in danger. Dignity is up for grabs. Honor is at risk. The risks involve confronting all of the deadly sins.

---

63. Weil, *Gravity and Grace*, 72.
64. Levan, *God Hates Religion*, 154.

One risks, however, because one is confident that all that is needed will come to those who embrace the quest. There is One who has gone before who said, "But seek first His kingdom and His righteousness; and all these things [needed] shall be added to you" (Matt 6:33).

Mary Wilcox's "developmental journey" parallels this idea of the quest as imaginative. The developmental journey is "a lifelong process of trying to make sense out of, and finding meaning in, our total environment. This environment includes things, people, moral issues: the objects of our logical thinking, our social perspective, and our moral reasoning. It also includes ways in which we try to put all this together."[65] Wilcox builds her theory of social perspective on the work of Lawrence Kohlberg and James Fowler. In her third and fourth stage of social perspective she articulates the concept of role-taking. Role-taking is the form of imaginative reflection whereby a person is able to enter into the inner thoughts and feelings of another. Role-taking is imaginative in that it seeks to place oneself in the situation of another person and, from that vantage point, interpret the thoughts and feelings of the other. Pastoral theology, understood as a quest for moral vision, requires the social perspective of role-taking.[66] This goes beyond empathy to enter into the worldview of the person, particularly to understand the suffering that he may be experiencing from his own vantage point.

Another aspect of the imaginative quest is the issue of resonance. In her work, *In a Different Voice*, Carol Gilligan urges us to embrace women's ways of perceiving and knowing as fresh paradigms that have important implications for the imaginative quest. Her research on the experiences of girls and women provides creative options not only for understanding gender differences, but also for seeing the world from the perspective of others. Her articulations of the theme of "voice" are especially noteworthy:

> People ask me what I mean by "voice." By voice I mean voice. Listen, I will say, thinking that in one sense the answer is simple. And then I will remember how it felt to speak when there was no resonance, how it was when I began writing . . . To have a voice

---

65. Wilcox, *Developmental Journey*, 224.

66. For a discussion of role-taking theory from the perspective of pastoral counseling, see Capps, *Biblical Approaches*, where he suggests that the Proverbs fall between third and fourth stage moral vision and are particularly useful for pre-marital counseling.

The Language of Moral Vision

is to be human. To have something to say is to be a person. But speaking depends on listening and being heard; it is an intensely relational act.[67]

This idea of voice and resonance is an important feature of the imaginative quest. The desire of pastoral theology is achieve a high degree of resonance with the suffering person. It is a matter of entering into the feelings of another to give voice to the deeper realities of suffering. Pastoral theology as moral vision is, therefore, a quest for understanding. It requires the social perspective of role-taking and the ability to articulate or voice the perspective of another in such a way that she will experience a resonance with that voice. To imagine what another is experiencing will go beyond empathy to enter into the thoughts and feelings of the other in such a way as to be able to express or articulate a resonant word.

A Quest Deepens and Illumines

Boisen's vision of what later came to be called "pastoral theology" inspires us toward a deeper compassion. It anticipates the blessing of standing with another in such a way as to be transformed. There is a tenacity of care that characterizes those who devote their lives to the parishes, hospitals, inner cities, prisons, and counseling centers throughout the world. In this tenacious passionate effort the pastor's vision is deepened and illumined. The deepening requires a reciprocal process of action and reflection.

John Patton introduces the existential phenomenologies of Maurice Merleau-Ponty and Paul Brockelman as a method for deepening our understanding of pastoral events, citing three insights from their writings.[68] The first involves understanding the world from the reference point of experience. As Brockelman points out,

> Rather than the world which we assume we "know" beforehand and which we use to explain our perceptual experience (sense impressions, etc.) it's actually the other way around: we can understand that "ideal" world of objects only in so far as we take a close look at our ordinary, bodily, perceptual experience.[69]

---

67. Gilligan, *Different Voice*, xvi.
68. Patton, *Ministry to Theology*, 13.
69. Brockelman, *Existential Phenomenology*, 55–56.

The second concerns pre-categorical perceptions. As Merleau-Ponty puts it, "When I focus on my immediate experience one of the first things I notice is that my experience to me as I live it through prior to reflection contains an implicit 'awareness.' The world is there before any possible analysis of mine."[70]

The third suggests that the purpose of reflection is to make explicit what is implicit in our experience. As Patton explains, "The purpose of reflection is to make explicit what has been until this point merely implicit within our experience. Existential phenomenology is an attempt to evoke and verbally articulate the various dimensions and elements of our prethematic, ordinary, and lived experience or 'existence.'"[71]

Patton uses existential phenomenology as a deepening method for students in pastoral training. However, even without such formal understandings or apprehensions, such deepening occurs in the course of ordinary pastoral encounters. Many pastors have experienced the deepening that comes as a surprising element of sustained relationship. Eugene Peterson describes one of his own deepening encounters:

> And then one day while reading Ulysses, at about page 611, an earthquake opened a fissure at my feet and all my assumptions of ordinariness dropped into it. All those routines of the pastoral vocation suddenly were no longer "routines" . . . I saw now that I had two sets of story to get straight. I already knew the gospel story pretty well. I was a preacher, a proclaimer with a message . . . But this other set of stories, these stories of Leopold Bloom and Buck Milligan, Jack Tyndale and Mary Vaughn, Nancy Lion and Bruce MacIntosh, Olaf Odegaard and Abigail Davidson— I had to get these stories straight too . . . I find myself listening for nuances, making connections, remembering and anticipating, watching how the verbs work . . . watching for signs of atonement, reconciliation, sanctification.[72]

This deepening serves to illumine as well. The doctrines come to life, ageless meanings shine, ministry becomes tapestry. The deepening illumines in such a way that theology becomes art, serendipity. The poet pens the sonnet that enlightens the world with freedom. The soaring words take us on their wings.

---

70. Merleau-Ponty, *Phenomenology of Perception*, x.
71. Patton, *Ministry to Theology*, 37.
72. Peterson, *Unpredictable Plant*, 124–26.

Conclusion

The quest for moral vision is at the heart of the enterprise of pastoral theology. It is a quest demanding pursuit, pushing toward boundaries. It is imaginative, and deepens and illumines experience, here the experience of suffering. It begins with experience, involves reflection, and ends with experience, the experience of consent to being through suffering. The quest for moral vision involves vulnerability and risk as it seeks to articulate both the experience of suffering and the grounds for hope. It is informed throughout by absolute faith.

CULTIVATING MORAL VISION

Having explored the characteristics of the *quest* for moral vision, I now want to focus on the cultivation of moral vision. In a prayer entitled "Creating the Church of Tomorrow," Archbishop Oscar Romero observes, "We may never see the end results, but that is the difference between the master builder and the worker. We are the workers, not master builders; ministers, not messiahs. We are prophets of a future not our own." In recognizing that "we may never see the end results," Romero captures something of the paradox of moral vision. We *do* see something, but it is "incomplete." "We cannot do everything," he writes, "and there is a sense of liberation in realizing that. This enables us to do something and to do it very well. It may be incomplete, but it is a beginning, a step along the way." We act even though our actions are not everything. We move forward, if only by a step. "It helps, now and then, to step back and take a long view." The acquisition of the long view is the subject matter of this section on moral vision. How do we gain such a view? Where does one acquire a sense of the good that moves one along in the effort of planting "seeds that one day will grow"? Where does the moral compass that guides thoughtful interaction with a broken world come from?

Stories and Moral Vision

In *Sins of Omission*, S. Dennis Ford suggests that our approach to moral vision must be from the underside, from the perspective of moral indifference.[73] This proposal challenges us to reflect on the ways in which moral vision is developed and/or hindered. This may itself be seen as a reframing of ethical reflection in order to understand moral vision

---

73. Ford, *Sins of Omission*.

from a new perspective. Ford is troubled by a common problem encountered in ethical reflection: "The most persistent problem about ethics is that most people could not care less . . . In the same way that Albert Camus once suggested that considering suicide is the beginning point of philosophy, so too considering the mystery of our own indifference is the beginning point of ethics."[74] Ford refers to the sins of omission as "the invisible side of ethical reflection."[75] He suggests that, like the astronomer's study of black holes, indifference "can be detected only by observing what is not there, by seeing nothing where there should be something."[76] Thus, to understand what true moral vision looks like, we must be able to define the absences. The study of the absence of moral commitment and participation informs our understanding of the causes of moral indifference.

According to Ford, indifference is the "failure to see, acknowledge . . . and act" on behalf of others.[77] The failure to see and acknowledge is reinforced by myths that serve to support one's fundamental stance. Ford cites the "power of stories to inform the way we see and structure experience, including our moral experience."[78] Stories have power to reinforce our moral indifference, but they also have the power to counter it.

To illustrate the power of stories to support moral indifference, Ford discusses common myths that serve to reinforce such indifference in the moral life.[79] Take, for example, the commonly known "myth of success" or "rag-to-riches motif." In this particular myth, the classic depiction is of a poor, rural boy who "moves to the city and there—unaided by anything but his own initiative, hard work, pluck, and persistence—overcomes obstacle after obstacle until success is his."[80] This myth reinforces the innate conviction that progress and growth are limitless. It frames the moral situation in such a way as to emphasize the advantages

74. Ibid., 11.
75. Ibid., 14.
76. Ibid., 15.
77. Ibid., 17.
78. Ibid., 53.
79. Ford defines myth rather broadly as "anything that serves as a model for the orientation of understanding, behavior, or attitude." He clarifies this position stating: "I use the term myth broadly here, to refer not only to traditional sacred stories but also to narratives, presumptions, concepts, ideologies, and popular entertainment as well." Ibid., 17.
80. Ibid., 54.

and to de-emphasize the disadvantages of the situation. Myths function most powerfully, says Ford, "when they are accepted unwittingly."[81]

Following the reasoning of the myth, poverty is not a real situation and the poor must simply be persons who have not applied themselves and therefore have not taken advantage of the infinite opportunities that lie before them. Likewise, the myth of success implies a basic fairness, suggesting that every participant has an equal footing and that no participant is disadvantaged in any way. The myth of success "ignores," in Ford's view, "what, in more reflective moments, may be obvious. We do not all start the race equally; some are more intelligent or gifted than others, some come from more supportive and loving families, some have more economic and social advantages."[82] The myth reinforces indifference by the compelling elements of the story that draw attention away from the obvious moral complexities of the situation. The myth resolves all of the tensions, inconsistencies, and inequities of a moral situation. Seen in this way, myths serve to reinforce indifference by validating the perceptions of reality that a person already has and leaving them unchanged.

Returning for a moment to the discussion of reframing method, a similarity in regards to *two levels of change* proposed by the method may be noted. *First-order change* is change that "occurs within a given system which itself remains unchanged."[83] In first order change, "The more things change, the more things stay the same."[84] The myth of success and other such myths reinforce moral indifference. *Second-order change* is change "that alters the system itself. In this type of change everything is different because the system itself is no longer the same."[85] The poem/parable word-form may be associated with second order change, thus functioning opposite to myth. While myths serve to reinforce indifference, the poem/parable re-forms the moral posture. While myths are morally numbing, the poem/parable is morally compelling. While myths have the effect of reducing moral commitment by confirming perceptions, the poem/parable seeks to follow the pattern of orientation, disorientation, and reorientation. The parable/poem, as illustrated in Peterson's experience of reading Ulysses, follows a pattern of perceptual

81. Ibid., 18.
82. Ibid., 57.
83. Capps, *Reframing*, 12.
84. Ibid.
85. Ibid.

disorientation and reorientation. The poems/parables have the capacity to undo our myths by reorienting us to the moral situation in a way that allows us to perceive something new. They re-form our moral posture by agitating in just the right place and allowing us to see something from a completely different frame of reference. While the myth reinforces what we believe and are already convinced of, the parable/poem probes our allegiances and prods us to understand the situation in a new light.

Jesus' parable of the Good Samaritan is one example. How is this parable designed to break down indifference? Several elements of re-framing are evident in the design of the parable. There is the fact that a despised Samaritan is the one who helps. There is the unexpected contrast between the compassion of the Samaritan for a Jewish traveler and the preoccupation and apathy of the priest and the Levite who are supposed to be ambassadors of God's work and proclaimers of the good news of the kingdom. Thus, the parable does more than advocate doing good to one's neighbor. It disorients by envisioning the help coming from a man who is the mortal enemy of the man who lies bleeding in the ditch. The parable acts in precisely the opposite way of the myth. Rather than reinforcing the dimensions of the story that are obvious ("we should do good to our friends"), the parable recites the story in such a way that everything may be seen in a different way ("we are to help our enemies too"). In this way, moral vision is deepened to become consent to being itself, not merely to one's own particular allegiances and favorite causes.

The Role of Experience in Moral Vision

Ford continues his treatment of the problem of indifference with a remarkable statement about the role of experience in moral vision. He states that "experience provides the basis for seeing."[86] What this means is that experience may have a formative role in the development of moral vision. If Ford is correct, then our starting point in understanding the relationship of suffering and virtue may be in the experiences of suffering and the expressions that result from these experiences. To clarify and expand on this point, Ford suggests that there are two kinds of experience. The first is primary or "real experience." Here he uses John Dewey's concept of aesthetic experience that is essentially sensory. In this view, "experience occurs whenever we are challenged to see new things, or

---

86. Ford, *Sins of Omission*, 85.

alternatively, to see old things in a new way."[87] Experience is an encounter with something real; it is "bumping against something not ourselves."[88] Such sensory experience, which Edwards terms "the sense of the heart," is the basis for all moral seeing. As Joan Erikson notes: "When the phrase 'to sense' is used, it means that all the senses are being tapped for information and that this results in what we call 'perception.' It is important to realize that all knowledge begins with sensory experience."[89]

The other kind of experience Ford identifies is "imagination." He notes that we may form experiences "because of an encounter with imaginative works of literature or art."[90] We are "inspired" by imaginative works that enable us to experience a situation vicariously. In this respect, "We often do what we first do in our imaginations; we often see what we first have seen through imaginative literature."[91] Our ability to experience a situation vicariously through art, music, drama, or literature is an important contributor to an appropriately moral vision. This imaginative form of experience is no less real than the sensory encounter. Moreover, the vicarious experiences elicited by the arts may in fact point back to sensory experiences in one's personal journey.

Moral vision, therefore, is always based on experience, whether the sensory experience of encounter or vicariously by the participation of imagination. In this respect, I have argued for the poetic word-form as an experience-near expression in which the words participate in the realities to which they point. The poem/parable form both includes the sensory experiences of suffering and expresses the moral vision to which they give rise. Great works of art, literature, and so on may be seen finally as eliciting vicarious experience that deepens and illumines the moral quest, and that challenges the received myths of moral indifference.

To fully develop these themes, and to address the problem that vicarious experience may touch the emotions but fail to activate a moral response, would entail a much more extensive discussion than can be developed here. My primary aim, however, has been to make a connection between Ford's assertion that "experience provides the basis" for moral seeing and the role of the poem/parable word-form in deepening

87. Ibid., 86.
88. Ibid.
89. Erikson, *Wisdom and the Senses*, 25.
90. Ibid., 88.
91. Ibid.

and illuminating moral vision. I have especially argued for the use of experience-near language to formulate conceptions of moral vision. I have also argued that the poem/parable functions in such vision in a diametrically opposite manner to that of morally numbing myths.[92]

---

92. By way of illustration, see Appendix C, "The Seven Days of Virtue," a creative exercise of moral reflection that combines autobiography and the poem/parable. It is framed on the premise that moral vision is best expressed as an imaginative response to the complex nuances of suffering and virtue.

4

A Constructive Proposal

Virtue and Pastoral Theology

THIS CHAPTER PRESENTS AN understanding of a pastoral theology of virtue in terms of the relational ontology of Jonathan Edwards. Though Edwards, himself a pastor, failed in many ways to incorporate his concept of virtue into his own pastoral work, his philosophical/theological construct of virtue is not for that reason discredited. I believe, moreover, that his relational ontology of virtue may be expanded, or, rather, focused, in a way he seems not to have envisioned, by viewing compassion as the crucial element in a theology of virtue that concerns itself with the experience of suffering.

The roots of the word compassion in Latin are *pati* "to suffer" and *cum* "with." "To suffer with" is to participate in the anxiety of suffering as a form of consent to another human being. This is true virtue. Such actions are not only related to but spring from God's own activity in the world, which is itself rooted in compassion. As Dietrich Bonhoeffer writes, "only the suffering God can help."[1]

PASTORAL THEOLOGY AND THE MORAL LIFE

In his effort to strengthen the theoretical foundations of pastoral theology, Don Browning has long advocated attention to what he has termed "the moral context of pastoral care."[2] For Browning, the formative starting point of pastoral theology is its rootedness in the Judeo-Christian ethic. Pastoral theology needs to be defined in terms of this particular moral context. Hence, "Pastoral theology should rediscover itself as a dimension of theological or religious ethics. It is the primary task of

1. Bonhoeffer, *Letters*, 361.
2. Browning, *Moral Context*, 130.

pastoral theology to bring together theological ethics and the social sciences to articulate a normative vision of the human life cycle."[3]

At first reading it may seem that I am advancing Browning's proposal. A theoretical proposal of virtue for pastoral theology seems to follow naturally from his assertion that pastoral theology ought to "rediscover itself as a dimension of theological or religious ethics." While I am sympathetic to the insight that pastoral theology is rooted in the Judeo-Christian ethic, I do not share the view that this ethic ought to be considered as the starting point of pastoral theology. I am rather inclined to agree with James Lapsley who points out that the critical question is whether moral inquiry constitutes the "foreground or the background"[4] of pastoral theology as a discipline. In my view it must certainly take the background.

What stands, then, at the foreground of pastoral theology? Rodney J. Hunter offers a helpful description of pastoral theology by identifying seven principal features of the "clinical pastoral perspective:"[5]

1. It sees life from "below."

2. It focuses on human situations in their personal and interpersonal dimension.

3. It seems to be concerned with what might be termed "the priority of being" over "doing."

4. It gives special attention to ambiguity, depth, and mystery.

5. It represents commitment to "concreteness," in contrast to conceptual abstraction.

6. It is irreducibly religious and ethical.

7. It gives a certain priority to the language of symbol, myth, dialogue, and story over the language of science, philosophy, theology, and technical practicality.

3. Browning, "Pastoral Theology," 24.

4. Hunter, "Future of Pastoral Theology," 63. Here Hunter merely cites Lapsley's contribution to the forum on the future of pastoral theology as a discipline.

5. Hunter, "What Is Pastoral about Pastoral Theology," 42–46. I think that the inclusion of the word "clinical" here is unfortunate in that it limits, in ways I suspect that Hunter does not wish to limit, the scope of his insights. I would simply use the term "pastoral theology" since I believe that Hunter has captured the essence of the enterprise with these seven features. His description here deserves further attention from the field.

In a related article, Hunter argues for viewing pastoral theology as a "form of practical knowledge" of "how to care for human beings."[6] Such an understanding of the discipline advances Seward Hiltner's original insight that "pastoral theology is an operation-centered discipline in the shepherding perspective."[7] It is also closely akin to the everyday notion of the "wisdom of experience."[8] Hiltner emphasizes that the term "experience" may be seen in a deeper sense from the "more common existentialist meaning . . . where it tends to be identified with the moment of consciousness."[9]

What, then, is the term "wisdom of experience" meant to convey? Hunter answers:

> In this connection it may be noted that this meaning of the word "experience" . . . suggests a form of knowledge that has accrued and matured through a history of practical, contingent events. It may also be noted that the Bible includes a large if somewhat neglected literature of practical knowledge, or wisdom, of this kind, which seems to have moved historically from being simply a collection of astute maxims and proverbs to theological intuitions and speculations of remarkable proportion and importance for later religious tradition.[10]

From this, Hunter turns to the particular question of specifically religious practical knowledge. He muses, "One might well wonder what sort of wisdom can be gained about how to live at the very boundaries of human experience."[11] Nonetheless, this is, in his view, essentially what authentic pastoral theology attempts.

With this insight Hunter moves us very close to the essential core of the pastoral theological enterprise. Unlike Browning, who attempts to extend pastoral theology into mainstream philosophy and ethics, Hunter conceives the primary aim of pastoral theology as "how to live transcendently as a child of God."[12] This is not a narrow pietism but a practical knowledge that "can be as profound and significant as

6. Hunter, "Future of Pastoral Theology," 65.
7. Hiltner as cited in ibid., 65, 66.
8. Hitner as cited in ibid., 67.
9. Hiltner as cited in ibid.
10. Ibid.
11. Ibid., 68.
12. Ibid., 69. Notably, Hunter does include the ethical dimension in his sixth point.

descriptive insight into reality or visions of the good, with which in any case it is intimately related."[13] He concludes by noting the promise of such an approach to pastoral theology:

> Our society probably needs some broadening and deepening of its conceptions of methods of living and even methods of caring and curing. An approach to these practical concerns undertaken with religious seriousness and theological perspective may be precisely what is needed for helping our civilization develop more humanly rich and fulfilling traditions of the art of life, beyond the very superficial moral and religious methodologies that presently prevail.[14]

Throughout I have attempted to remain true to a vision of pastoral theology that takes "care" as its central motif. Care, however, is not a simple concept. The "practical knowledge" of how to care for others moves us to the very limits of human possibility. Hunter outlines the implications of this prioritizing of care for pastoral theology:

> Presumably a pastoral theology conceived along these lines would be concerned with developing practical religious knowledge about caring for others, that is, how to care for others in their concrete contingencies and problems so as to stimulate or enable their life of faith and practical knowledge of God.[15]

Perhaps the best way to address Hunter's question, "What sort of wisdom can be gained about how to live at the very boundaries of human experience?" is to notice the ways in which the acquisition of such wisdom is impeded. In other words, we begin with absences, not presences.

DISCERNING THE ABSENCES: SOME REFLECTIONS ON IMMATURE MORAL VISION

What makes for inauthenticity in virtue? This question raises the issue of motivation in the moral life. Motives elude scrutiny by external observation and function in a hidden manner in our life. Authentic virtue, however, is not easily persuaded by external stimuli. Applause and criticism have little effect on the life of virtue itself. True virtue neither seeks

---

13. Ibid.
14. Ibid.
15. Ibid.

the affirmation of others nor is it easily dissuaded by the condemning words of the critic.

Consider, for example, the virtue of humility. Reflection on the virtue of humility exposes the pseudo-types that might look like humility but nevertheless are exposed by the consequences of false motives. Self-castigation is not humility. In order to achieve the appearance of humility, the one who castigates herself allows others to rescue and restore the self-destructive tendency that gains recognition and comfort at once. The motive for castigation is self-pity, but worse, self-pity conceived to make oneself appear noble. This is not humility.

Deference is not humility. Deference is much closer to humility in that it demands a sincerity that acknowledges the presence of another who is worthy of honor or recognition. However, not all deference is noble. It may have the mixed motive of unwillingness to become vulnerable or open by refusing to extend one's gift to the needy and fragmented world. To defer when a talent lies buried in the sand as a consequence of fear is not humility but boredom. Such deference earns the favor of others even though gifts and talents are being withheld in selfish isolation. To the deferring talented the returning Master had not commendation but disgust (Matt 26:14–30).

Spiritual devotion is not humility. Here again, the subtle nuances of hidden and distorted motivations raise questions concerning the sincerity of pious activity. Giving all of one's possessions to the poor (surely a sign of true virtue), fasting and praying earnestly in the church or synagogue, and even the act of martyrdom are no sure signature of a humble disposition (1 Cor 13:1–3; Matt 6:1). Spiritual devotion and external piety may be a façade that bears little resemblance to true humility. Such attempts can be worthless religious actions.

Though self-castigation, deference, and spiritual devotion may be the expressions of a humble heart, they are not necessarily true signs of humility. In each instance, the deeper issue of motive is determinative, and motives require discernment. Authenticity in the moral life, therefore, requires discernment. All true virtues have parallel pseudo-virtues that imitate them. The question then becomes: how does the conscientious participant in the life of virtue discern whether his actions spring from an authentic consent to being? Authentic virtue requires discernment, that is, the capacity to ascertain and give one's consent to the authentic expression of God's presence repeated in time and space through persons sharing in God's expressed intentions. Authentic virtue is consent to being.

This illustration of pseudo-forms of humility suggests that, in order to formulate a constructive proposal of virtue in pastoral theology, the pseudo-types must first be exposed. Following Ford's idea in *Sins of Omission: A Primer on Moral Indifference* that the most constructive approach to ethics is through observing the "absences," I identify seven sins of omission in the common pursuit of virtue. These, in turn, provide an entry into a constructive vision of authentic virtue. The sevens sins of omission could be summarized as follows:

Prescribed Morality

Moral norms may serve societies to enhance life in ways that promote civility, order, and lawfulness, but they cannot instill virtue. Even if a citizen were to follow all of the moral prescriptions of her society without fail, this gives no assurance that virtue has occurred. Prescriptive morality demands obedience. It outlines the rigorous rules and regulations of cooperation that reward the faithful and punish the offender.

Few would deny the value of prescriptive morality in society. When governments disallow murder, curb violence, and dissuade mercenaries, they perform a necessary, constructive task. Similarly, churches do well to develop policies and procedures for the conduct of their members, and employers do well to outline criteria for the conduct, habits, and demeanor of their employees. However, prescribed morality is choiceless. Adherence to laws, rules, and constitutions may be a significant sign of good citizenry but it does not account for virtue, primarily because the compliance is demanded or coerced by power. Thus, prescribed morality identifies two of our absences: absence of true love for God and absence of freedom or choice.

Religious Piety

Piety is expressed through behaviors that are cultivated in the life of a religious community. In this sense they have an important function in the practice of religious life. Common activities associated with piety are prayer, the contribution of offerings, religious rituals (such as fasting, washing, etc.), a dress code, and observance of festivals or holy days. Piety is an essential ingredient to the honest practice of religion. Religious communities have deeply meaningful rituals that are often rooted in centuries of tradition and that sustain the life of the faith community in powerful ways. This does not mean, however, that authentic virtue is a function of religious piety. The question of motive comes to the surface once again precisely around this point. In Judeo-Christian thought, for example, some of the most scathing critiques in Scripture are reserved for those whose practice of external piety does not match the inner life of the heart in a true love for God.

Thus, religious piety may not serve authentic virtue. In fact, it may undermine it by the cultivation of religious activity that serves to reinforce one's sense of honest participation in the life of God while diminishing one's sensitivity to self-deception. The prophet Isaiah articulates God's offence at the inappropriate religious piety of the congregation:

> "What are your multiplied sacrifices to me?" says the Lord. "I have had enough of burnt offerings of rams, and the fat of fed cattle. And I take no pleasure in the blood of bulls, lambs, or goats. When you come to appear before Me, who requires of you this trampling of My courts? Bring your worthless offerings no longer, their incense is an abomination to Me. New moon and sabbath, the calling of assemblies—I cannot endure iniquity and the solemn assembly. I hate your new moon festivals and your appointed feasts, they have become a burden to me. I am weary of bearing them. So when you spread out your hands in prayer, I will hide My eyes from you, yes, even though you multiply your prayers, I will not listen. Your hands are full of bloodshed." (Isa 1:11–15; NASB)

The practice of religious piety accompanied by consent to injustice and actively contributing to the oppression of others is not only gravely inappropriate, it is an offence to God. A heart that is given over to the external practices of piety while ignoring the social responsibility of sharing in justice is self-deceived and elicits not the approval but the disgust of God who is weary of hypocrisy. This indictment of piety points out two further absences in the pursuit of authentic virtue: absence of a pure heart (Ps 24:4) and absence of a concern for social justice.

Obsessive Moralism

Morality that finds expression in obsessive and driven obligation does not promote authentic virtue. Often the obsession is rooted in judgmental attitudes that alienate the moralist from others. The driven spirit does not allow for critical reflection but reinforces moral absolutism that sustains the conviction of self-justification and allows the moralist to accuse others. The vicious circle of driven absolutism, judgment, and alienation is self-perpetuating. Obsessive moralism sustains obsessive moralism in an endless spiral of self-deception, animosity, and isolation.

Moralism is a particular problem in the search for authentic virtue because of its ability to sustain itself. The obsessive moralist requires no documentation, no proof, no critical insight to continue in a firmly held conviction. Attempts to confront the hubris that protects the obsession only elicit hostility. Attempts compassionately to disarm the hidden motives reinforcing the moralistic tendency lead to suspicion or even a more volatile reaction. Such obsessive moralism is often driven by religious fanaticism. However, all fanaticism, religious or otherwise, is prone to this tendency. Fanaticism promotes premature conclusions and eclipses one's ability to perceive accurately. It reinforces a sick belief system by the absence of critical reflection and an incapacity to discern the perspective of others. It therefore points to two more absences in the life of virtue: absence of perspective (the ability to see; moral vision), and absence of critical reflection (the ability to discern or judge according to wisdom).

Dislocated Abstraction

Abstractions that distance real encounters from conclusions associated with them function dislocatively, that is, they remove the experience from the truth of which it is a symbol. Dietrich Bonhoeffer expressed his view that abstractions, especially in the moral life, are out of place. He states, "the words are correct, but they have no weight."[16] He urges those who desire to pursue ethical insight to locate the truth in a time and a place, suggesting that "timeless and placeless ethics"[17] leads to weightless abstraction. Authentic virtue, therefore, must be located in experience, in the practical sphere of everyday life. It requires that we place our insights in the context of time and place and speak from the concrete experiences that give rise to them. The final absence is absence of concreteness.

---

16. Bonhoeffer, *Ethics*, 270.
17. Ibid.

Authentic virtue is not easily described. However, by observing some of the absences in common pursuits of the virtuous life we are able to isolate what is clearly not virtue. The following table outlines the seven absences that are apparent in an immature moral vision.

Tendencies	Absences
Prescribed Morality	1. The absence of love for God
	2. The absence of freedom
Religious Piety	3. The absence of a pure heart
	4. The absence of social justice
Obsessive Moralism	5. The absence of perspective
	6. The absence of critical reflection
Dislocated Abstraction	7. The absence of concreteness

IMPLICATIONS FOR A PASTORAL THEOLOGY OF VIRTUE

I have argued that the moral life of virtue is at the heart of the enterprise of pastoral theology. To show this in a graphic way, I have correlated the moral absences with Hunter's features of pastoral theology.[18] These correlations demonstrate that pastoral theology provides a valuable framework for thinking about virtue. Rather than assuming that a broader ethical framework is required for the development of a pastoral theology of virtue,[19] I am suggesting that the way pastoral theology is structured as a discipline already allows for inclusion of the dimensions of the moral life that are lacking in an immature moral vision. From this we may begin to see what some of the features of a construct of virtue for pastoral theology might be.

---

18. Hunter, "What Is Pastoral about Pastoral Theology," 42–46.

19. See Browning, "Pastoral Theology," where Browning insists that "Pastoral theology should understand itself as an expression of theological ethics, primarily concerned with the religio-ethical norms governing the human life cycle." Ibid., 30.

Hunter's Features of Pastoral Theology that Respond to the Moral Absences	Moral Absences in an Immature Moral Vision
Sees life from below	Absence of *perspective*
Focuses on *human situations* in their personal and *interpersonal* dimensions	Absence of *social justice*
Concern with the priority of "*being*" over "doing"	Absence of a *pure heart*
Gives special attention to *ambiguity*, *depth*, and *mystery*	Absence of *critical reflection*
Commitment to "*concreteness*"	Absence of *concreteness*
Irreducibly *religious* and ethical	Absence of *love for God*
Gives a certain priority to the language of *symbol*, *myth*, *dialogue*, and *story*	Absence of *freedom*

From the perspective provided by pastoral theology, we may begin to discern a positive vision of authentic virtue. The language of symbol, myth, dialogue, and story will be given priority to the prescribed teaching of religious moralism. Perspective will be drawn from "life below" rather than from the extractions of moralism. Love for God will ground a pastoral theology of virtue as a truly religious and ethical construct rather than as a function of prescribed morality. Attention to experience (primary and secondary) will ground ideas about authentic virtue in concreteness, not in moral abstraction. Critical reflection on the ambiguities, depth, and mystery of the moral life will replace the blind faith of obsessive moralism. Attention to character, to "being" over "doing," will confront the tendency of religious piety to act in the right ways but without a pure heart. The demand for social justice will be intrinsic to the vision of virtue in pastoral theology rather than the religious piety that pretends to care for the other but is actually preoccupied with religion.

IMAGES OF MINISTRY: A CONSTRUCTIVE PASTORAL THEOLOGY OF VIRTUE

Having established these correlations between a view of pastoral theology based on "religious practical knowledge" and an authentic moral vision, I now turn to the implications of this pastoral theology of virtue for the parish pastor. To this end, I will identify the images of ministry or "pastoral images" that are central to the pastoral theology of virtue that I have put forth. These images are the attentive poet, the weeping prophet, and the good shepherd. While I recognize that there are many other images of ministry that have informed pastoral identity throughout the history of the church, these three are especially congruent with the pastoral theology of virtue set forth here. They especially give concrete form to what Edwards himself envisioned in his treatise on the nature of true virtue. They are the pastoral dimensions, as it were, of the consent to being.

The image of the attentive poet captures the pastoral features of critical reflection, concreteness, and freedom. The image of the weeping prophet captures the features of perspective and social justice, while the image of the good shepherd features a pure heart and love for God.

The Attentive Poet

CRITICAL REFLECTION

According to Hunter, one feature of a mature pastoral theology is that it "gives special attention to ambiguity, depth, and mystery."[20] Pastoral theology is comfortable with depth, with ambiguity, and with mystery. Our participation in the complex dynamics of human encounter resists an easy classification of persons, values, ideas, concepts, or experiences. In fact, as a discipline, our work requires us to attempt to speak with conviction about these very ambiguities. There is a need, I have suggested, for pastors to make use of the parabolic language of the poem, which attends to the nuances of these mysteries. Through such language, one is enabled to enter the abyss of suffering with others and, then, in solidarity with them, to begin to articulate those experiences in appropriate ways. Rubem Alves suggests that this attentiveness requires both an

---

20. Ibid., 44.

attention to the Wind of God (Hebrew *ruach*, spirit),[21] the brokenness in the world,[22] and the suffering in our own heart. [23] Such attention, says Simone Weil, is prayer.[24] Pastoral care has long recognized the ministry of prayer as a form of healing the inner spirit.[25] What is required, as we cultivate this skill, is deeper attention to the sufferings of others and the resonances within our own heart that provide what Nouwen calls "sensitive articulation."[26]

Sensitive articulation is the skill of the attentive poet. When she speaks, those who listen can say: "You say what I suspected, you express what I vaguely felt, you bring to the fore what I fearfully kept in the back of my mind. Yes, yes—you say who we are, you recognize our condition . . ."[27] The conceptual framework upon which the attentive poet builds her word-forms is the objective presence of virtue as an ontological reality that she accepts by faith. This is not a fantasy or something essentially subjective but is rather the compassion of God infinitely repeated in time and space. In order to discern the words that might be helpful, the pastor trains herself to listen to the sufferings of others, the ambiguities in her own heart, and the gentle movements of the breeze of God's Spirit. The word-forms take us on their flights to Beauty.[28]

Aesthetic theology and pastoral care are intimately related in this matter of attentive language. Pastoral care is the attempt to word the Void, to capture and express the ultimate anxieties and the sublime hopes that wrestle for supremacy in our hearts. Such expression implies participation in suffering itself. For, as Tillich emphasizes, "in order to offer such meaningful expression one must be immersed in ultimate reality."[29] Only by our own immersion in the structures of life itself are

---

21. Alves, *Poet, Warrior, Prophet*, 137.
22. Ibid., 134.
23. Ibid., 140.
24. Weil, *Gravity and Grace*, 170.
25. On the idea of "blessing," see Hulme, *Pastoral Care and Counseling*, chapter 7, "Prayer in Pastoral Counseling," 23–25.
26. Nouwen, *Wounded Healer*, 39.
27. Ibid.
28. In this regard, Alves, *Poet, Warrior, Prophet*, 125, states, "The human being unconsciously composes life's score according to the laws of beauty, even in the moments of deepest despair."
29. Tillich, *Theology of Culture*, 65.

we able to begin to speak about the dimensions that are opened up by the words we use.

Several word-forms are made available to the pastor for the caring enterprise. The lament, with its psalmic language of protest, is useful to express the groanings of those who suffer. As Soelle says, the first step toward overcoming suffering is by protesting it in the form of the lament.[30] The parable has also been recommended as the primary word-form to be used by the attentive poet. The modern word-form for parable is the poem. Poetry is recommended as one way to express the world-disclosing truths experienced in the pastoral encounter. The poem/parable is meant to break through. It shapes us and interprets us. It re-forms us from the inside—shaping who we are and how we see our world. The word-form of the poem/parable changes our moral posture in the world. Unlike the myth, which reinforces what we already see (first order change), the poem/parable reframes the situation in such a way as to allow us to see life from a different angle (second order change). The place where this touches our moral vision is not simply a reorientation but rather a "reformation" or inner change in moral posture to the world.

The attentive poet's task is to express the words that come from meaningful pastoral encounter. On the supposition that such word-forms would assist not only the parishioner but also the pastor in her search for ultimate meaning, this skill is recommended as part of the repertoire of the serious pastor. Thus, one link to virtue that the image of the attentive poet reflects is the attention to ambiguity, depth, and mystery, hence, poetry as critical reflection. Discernment may be understood in this light. Bernard Haring recommends "the virtue of criticism," noting: "The word criticism comes from the Greek *krinein* meaning 'to judge' or 'to discern.' This restoration of the true sense of criticism will happen if we are willing to let ourselves be challenged by prophetic-critical men and women."[31] Therefore, the pastor, as attentive poet, discerns, in critical reflection, the nuances of the moral life and the possible meanings of the depth dimension. When unable to articulate these fully, we may at least "say what the situation is."[32] The words we use, as symbols,

---

30. Soelle, *Suffering*, 70. On the use of lament psalms in grief counseling, see Capps, *Biblical Approaches*, chapter 2.

31. Haring, *Virtues*, 70.

32. Soelle, *Suffering*, 70.

open up what Tillich calls "the hidden level of reality."[33] Precisely here, at the ontological level, suffering and virtue meet. Moreover, if virtue is "consent to being" as Edwards suggests, then our attempts to express the moral dimensions of reality require our entire participation: mind, heart, and will.

Concreteness

The second feature of mature pastoral theology is a "commitment to 'concreteness,' in contrast to conceptual abstraction."[34] In pastoral theology, says Hunter, we must attend "first and finally, as a matter of methodological principle and practice, to real, concrete, particular human beings and human situations, and hold ourselves accountable to their stubborn but colorful reality."[35] Pastoral theology takes seriously the experiences and encounters of day-to-day life. The pastor, as pastoral theologian, recognizes that the compilation of experiences makes up the very fabric of life in all of its complexity. A pastoral theology of virtue, therefore, will not be given to abstraction or mere moral speculation. It will be rooted, rather, in the observations that arise from day-to-day encounters in real life. It gives preference to experience as the beginning point in all reflection, including theological reflection.

In this respect we have noted that, in Edwards's description of true virtue, there are two elements that ground his work in experience. First, his own experience of conversion was an important factor shaping his moral vision. Throughout his lifetime he reflected on the experience of tasting God's glory and majesty, which ultimately led him to develop a conception of God as Beauty over against theological ideas of God as Power.[36] This personal experience was combined with his special interest in the religious experiences of his parishioners and others affected by the revivals in New England. Second, Edwards uses Locke's epistemology to convey the idea of sensory experience as a primary and formative power in the moral life. Edwards's conception of "the sense of the heart"

---

33. Tillich, *Theology of Culture*, 59.
34. Hunter, "What Is Pastoral about Pastoral Theology," 45.
35. Ibid.
36. Delattre, "Beauty and Theology," 145. Delattre concludes, "Beauty, goodness, and power may be taken as representative of the three kinds of divine perfections into which all of them may be resolved, according to this formulation. And their rank among the divine perfections is first beauty, then goodness, then power, in descending order."

moves away from speculative knowledge (of which he was suspicious) to a more complete knowledge that promotes the affections and the will toward the nature of reality itself, effecting "that consent, propensity and union of heart to being in general, which is immediately exercised in a general good will" (true virtue).[37]

A pastoral theology of virtue, therefore, will remain true to the fundamental approach that Edwards outlined. Pastoral theologians will continue to enter into Boisen's abyss to attend to the experiences of the suffering, finding ways to relate these experiences to the conceptions of the good life and the presence of God in the world. The primary work of pastoral theology will always be to take seriously the nature of experience and, following Edwards's lead, will develop a thoughtful epistemological framework within which these experiences may be understood.

The experience-near nature of pastoral work entails a commitment to concreteness. Gustavo Gutierrez recommends a rejection of any "way of theologizing that does not take account of concrete situations, of the sufferings and hopes of human beings."[38] This may also be said of a mature pastoral theology of virtue. We cannot be content with abstractions, with lofty theological language, or with philosophical frameworks if they do not reflect the anxieties, the pains, and the cries of anguish of the human experience. Of such lofty language and systems, Bonhoeffer's comment that "the words are correct but they have no weight"[39] is a telling, withering condemnation.

Virtue, then, must be understood in the fragments of experience of the broken lives we live. Moral formation, from the perspective of a mature pastoral theology of virtue, is rooted in the concrete experiences of consent that take place in the depths of the human soul. Such a pastoral theology does not try to explain such experiences completely but rather serves to facilitate their occurrence and repetition. In this sense a pastoral theology of virtue is a commitment to hope. It is the hope that persons can and will change. Such change, though occasionally spawned by radical upheavals, generally happens in complex movements of the soul's interior and can be nurtured by prayer, encouragement (putting courage into), and by way of moral exemplars.

---

37. Edwards, *True Virtue*, 3.
38. Gutierrez, *On Job*, 29.
39. Bonhoeffer, *Ethics*, 270.

Once again, the attentive poet is called upon to articulate the sufferings of the soul. Kierkegaard asks:

> What is a poet? A poet is an unhappy being whose heart is torn by secret sufferings, but whose lips are so strangely formed that when the sighs and the cries escape them, they sound like beautiful music...And men crowd about the poet and say to him: "Sing for us soon again;" that is as much as to say: "May new sufferings torment your soul, but may your lips be formed as before; the cries would only frighten us, but the music is delicious."[40]

The pastor is the attentive poet. In *The Poet's Gift*, Donald Capps has demonstrated the similarities between the poet and the pastor. Both the poet and the pastor share a common passion for honest reflection on life's deepest meanings; both the poet and the pastor strive towards the integration of head and heart; both share a preference for language that is "experience-near," and both exhibit a deep care for words.[41]

Freedom

A third feature of a mature pastoral theology is that it "gives a certain priority to the language of symbol, myth, dialogue and story."[42] Unlike those who follow the moralistic tendencies of prescribed virtue, the pastor as attentive poet is willing to participate as one who tells his own story. Vulnerability is a key ingredient in pastoral theology because of the pastor's willingness to make her "own wounds"[43] available as "a source of healing." The pastor's use of autobiography may assist in this venture of truth-telling from the experiences of "suffering with" others. The attentive poet may not be able to explain the source of suffering or answer the question why, but may at least "say what the situation is." The telling of the story of one's own compelling quest into suffering is an important dimension of a pastoral theology of virtue.

This is in contrast to the kind of moral speaking that attempts to offer answers without a willingness to participate in the quest. Life is approached not so much on the basis of its questions but as a journey or a quest into the unknown, uncharted waters of suffering. Authentic virtue always has this ability to move into the depths. Language is used

40. As cited by Kreeft, *Making Sense out of Suffering*, 75.
41. Capps, *The Poet's Gift*, 3, 4.
42. Hunter, "What Is Pastoral about Pastoral Theology," 46.
43. Nouwen, *Wounded Healer*, 88.

symbolically to express something deeper to which it points. The attentive poet uses the words without really knowing the full expression of their meaning. The poet knows that detached observation, calculating analysis, and dry hypotheses fail to break through. What is needed are word-forms that express the depth dimension of reality and open up the soul[44]—the language of poetry.

The work in pastoral care of attentive listening and sensitive articulation is an important dimension of authenticity. Nouwen quotes Carl Rogers on precisely this point of what an important thing it is to learn in pastoral theology:

> I have found that the very feeling which has seemed to me most private, most personal and hence most incomprehensible by others, has turned out to be an expression for which there is a resonance in many other people. It has led me to believe that what is most personal and unique in each one of us is probably the very element which would, if it were shared or expressed, speak most deeply to others. This has helped me to understand artists and poets who have dared to express the unique in themselves.[45]

Freed from the masks of prescribed morality, the attentive poet is able to speak most honestly about the depths of experience in ways that create a resonance in others. This mutual resonance and the subsequent harmony that comes with it ties Edwards's ontological concept of virtue with the experiences of the soul and the articulation of these experiences in a language that tells the truth about the situation.

One of the disappointments of Edwards's own pastoral ministry was his inability to escape the prescribed morality of his day in order to function as the attentive poet with his own parishioners. Yet, this is surely a problem that other pastors have experienced. It seems indigenous to the soil of pastoral ministry. Pastors often experience themselves as lacking freedom, not unlike caged animals, in this regard. This is one of the challenges of the attentive poet; not only to attend to the sufferings of the community and the internal strivings of one's own heart, but also to find a way to freedom without becoming "worldless." Such freedom will be reflected in the pastor's capacity to speak the truth genuinely in such a way that others will be able to say: "You say what I suspected, you express what I vaguely felt, you bring to the fore what I fearfully kept in

---

44. Tillich, *Theology of Culture*, 57.
45. Rogers, *On Becoming a Person*, 26 (emphasis added).

the back of my mind. Yes, yes,—you say who we are, you recognize our condition..."[46]

The attentive poet, therefore, fulfils three functions of a mature pastoral theology of virtue. Through poetry as critical reflection he gives special attention to the ambiguities, depths, and mysteries of life. His word-forms demonstrate a commitment to concreteness and avoid the speculative abstraction of moral philosophy. Further, he gives priority to the language of symbol, myth, dialogue, and story over the masked words of prescribed morality. As attentive poet, the pastor speaks words that resonate and works from a posture where beauty replaces duty as the gauge of the moral life.

The Weeping Prophet

Perspective

A fourth feature of a mature pastoral theology is that it "sees life from below... in the sense of focusing principally on the aspects of hurt, need, conflict, and failure present in every human situation... As pastoral theologians we have a vocation, as it were, to zero in on human pain and brokenness."[47] Here, Hunter uses the language of perspective to express this dimension of pastoral theology. It is a matter of viewing life "from below," of taking a certain posture in the world and expressing things from that viewpoint. To capture this dimension in a pastoral image, I turn to the image of the weeping prophet. The prophetic image is one that calls for a certain perspective. The prophetic voice is not able to speak on behalf of others authentically until there has been a complete participation in the life with others. Prophetic speaking requires participation in the life of the brokenness that is the human condition.

Compassion, meaning "to suffer with," is an integrative motif for the prophetic perspective. It involves a participation in the brokenness of the world and speaks prophetically from the perspective of the woundedness that we all share. This perspective of compassion is the particular contribution that pastoral theology brings to discussions of virtue in moral philosophy. As I have contended, Edwards's theological construct of consent to being is preferable to other ideas of the nature of virtue itself. Following Edwards, we may formulate a construct of virtue

---

46. Nouwen, *Wounded Healer*, 39.
47. Hunter, "What Is Pastoral about Pastoral Theology," 42.

structured ontologically on the premise that it is God's compassion infinitely repeated in time and space to which our hearts consent when we are seeking the right way of being and the right way of acting. In Edwards's scheme, these moments of consent make for the life of virtue itself. Consent to being means consent to and with God's active compassion in a broken world. Consent to being means participating in the suffering of others by our active presence in the moment of their suffering. Consent to being also means to participate fully in our own suffering, to drink the cup of bitterness that is ours as well.

The weeping prophet not only weeps with others in search of hope but also weeps with God. Though it is beyond the scope of this work, I would contend that Edwards's construct of virtue has value for speaking about the suffering of God, a difficult issue in theology. Consider, for example, Moltmann's idea of "forsakenness." Moltmann here attempts, I think, to outline the way in which our own experiences of forsakenness are ontologically related to the suffering of Christ and to the life of God within the Trinity. Hence, he notes, "those who are forsaken are already taken up by Christ's forsakenness into Divine history."[48]

The weeping prophet speaks from below. With a radical commitment to those who are suffering, pastoral theology is one of the unique places where the voice of the weeping prophet will be cultivated. But moral vision is also an important, related aspect of the weeping prophet's function. This is connected with the particular solidarity that comes from staying in the situation of suffering compassionately. From this vantage point there is not only a new perspective being offered but a new ability to debunk the myths that serve to reinforce indifference. This function of exposing myths and breaking down their power to seduce us into moral complacency is an important aspect of the weeping prophet's function in the pursuit of virtue. Such moral vision comes from a posture of "suffering with," which is often termed "solidarity." Bryan Stone states, "The ability to expose oppressive myths and powers requires a solidarity with victims that provides *a perspective from below*."[49]

I have followed Ford in his contention that experience is the basis of moral seeing. In this connection, I included Moltmann's autobiographical experiences, and suggested that his own experience of "forsakenness" helps to account for the theological vision that he later articulated as a

---

48. Moltmann, *Crucified God*, 255.
49. Stone, *Compassionate Ministry*, 122 (emphasis added).

desire to be a "theologian of hope,"⁵⁰ one whose hope is rooted in the fact that Christ, the forsaken one, also speaks from below on our behalf. The compassionate participation in the life of brokenness, which is the human condition, places this prophetic task in the very center of the pastoral role. The pastor, as weeping prophet, shares with others in the enormous pain of their suffering and expresses "from below" the protest that, in the end, is simply a variation on a theme: "My God, why have you forsaken me?"

Social Justice

A mature pastoral theology "focuses on human situations in their personal and interpersonal dimensions."⁵¹ Pastoral theology has been criticized at times for focusing on the situation of the individual without paying close attention to the broader social constructs that are affecting the dynamics of the situation. In recent years, there has been a shift toward a deeper integration of these other dimensions of the human situation. Hunter and Patton state that "under the impact of contextual and social concerns, pastoral care and counseling's operational theological tradition is now at a point where . . . the field is beginning to 'widen its horizons.'"⁵² The weeping prophet is concerned for social justice. This posture is in radical opposition to the type of religious piety that claims moral purity while neglecting or even facilitating social injustice. Recognizing the interconnectedness of all human situations, the weeping prophet has a broader commitment to the well-being of others.

I have argued that Edwards's aesthetic theology envisions the moral life in a dynamic relational ontology. By defining virtue as "consent to being," Edwards places the sequence of moral activity in the arena of our interactions with one another and with God. I have stated that for him, love for God and love for neighbor are not viewed separately but are dimensions of an entire dynamic relational vision of the moral life. In this respect, a mature pastoral theology of virtue will understand the moral life not from the perspective of private virtues being lived out in isolation but from the perspective of our interconnectedness. This may be one way to overcome the problems raised by moral philosophy concerning the unity of the virtues. Are the virtues one or many? In Edwards's

---

50. Moltmann, *Theology of Hope*.
51. Hunter, "What Is Pastoral about Pastoral Theology," 42.
52. Hunter and Patton, "Commitments," 39, 40.

scheme the individual virtues are always related to true virtue, which is consent to being. Ultimately, true virtue occurs when we as human beings align our perspective on the moral issues with God's compassionate participation in the world demonstrated as mercy.

A deliberate concern for social justice forms the very fabric of the moral life itself. It is not optional but essential to a dynamic conception of the moral life. The life of virtue, then, needs to be understood as a multiplicity of relations of justice. Consent to being reflects a general good will taking into account the social complexion of the moral life. The weeping prophet is committed to social justice. This is an integral part of the pastor's authentic role in the community. In order to fulfill this role in pastoral theology, Roy SteinhoffSmith suggests that the idea of "care" itself be refined to include these broader dimensions: "Care is the activity of a person or a community that supports the full and powerful participation in communities and societies of those who are suffering, excluded, objectified, or oppressed."[53] The weeping prophet, we have said, offers such care in the context of both suffering and hope. His stance is one of hopefulness in the context of a suffering world. From this vantage point the weeping prophet is enraged by oppression and works diligently for liberation. There is at once a call to solidarity and a call to hope. The mutism of suffering is overcome as the lament of the community is expressed, prompting actions of protest against the injustices that caused them.[54]

Weeping prophets work for the good. They are not interested simply in understanding suffering. They are intentionally participating in the liberating power of the gospel in a broken world. James Cone, whose own participation in social justice work is widely known, states: "Christians are called to suffer with God in the fight against evil in the present age ... This vocation is not a passive endurance of injustice but, rather, a political and social praxis of liberation in the world."[55] The weeping prophet functions as leaven in a world that needs healing. His concern is not only for the individual cases of extreme suffering but for the ways that those particular sufferings are connected to the entire fabric of injustice and oppression. Justice and freedom, then, become the locus of concern for the weeping prophet. While recognizing that justice is the ultimate goal

---

53. SteinhoffSmith, "Politics of Pastoral Care," 148.
54. Soelle conveys these three phases of overcoming suffering in *Suffering*, 73.
55. Cone, *God of the Oppressed*, 177.

to which Christians are committed, Donald Capps points to freedom as an interim objective in pastoral care's renewed concern for liberation. He says that "freedom is what enables us to experience life as a web, not a tether, much less a chain. And pastoral care involves the capacity to hear—to listen for—the other's cry for release from one or more prisons of human devising."[56]

The Good Shepherd

A Pure Heart

A mature pastoral theology will demonstrate "a concern for 'being' over 'doing.'"[57] The kind of person we are affects our moral vision and our ability to demonstrate compassion. Authentic virtue needs to be seen as derivative of a state of character or a moral posture in the world. I have noted that virtue ethics emphasizes being over doing and have suggested that such an approach to the moral life deepens our ability to conceive how one might facilitate moral development in the life of persons. The pastoral image of the good shepherd is especially relevant here. The image of the pastor as shepherd has a longstanding and enduring place in the Christian tradition. It has also been central to pastoral theology, which has emphasized the caring features of Christian ministry over its other features (preaching the gospel, witnessing the faith to unbelievers, educating the faithful, etc.) While recognizing the problematic features of the image, Alastair Campbell suggests that the idea of the shepherd's courage might be the focus of its renewal in pastoral care. This redirects the shepherding motif from what he perceives as the weaker image of "tender and solicitous concern"[58] offered by Hiltner toward the "tougher" dimensions of pastoral care that are "costly, unsettling, even distasteful at times."[59]

Though I am sympathetic to Campbell's effort to emphasize the risk dimensions of the shepherding task, his image of the courageous shepherd does not, in my judgment, go far enough. In particular, I have emphasized throughout this book that the life of virtue has important bearing on all dimensions of pastoral work. Therefore, the motif of

---

56. Capps, *The Poet's Gift*, 170.
57. Hunter, "What Is Pastoral about Pastoral Theology," 43.
58. Campbell, *Rediscovering Pastoral Care*, 43.
59. Ibid., 36.

"good" shepherd includes Campbell's "virtue" of courage, but we need, in addition, to incorporate all the virtues in the pursuit of authentic pastoral involvement. Not just courage but also wisdom, kindness, mercy, hope, fidelity, and many others are aspects of the shepherding role.

Here, again, Edwards is especially instructive. If we are to frame the shepherding role as a participation in what is essentially good, we need a conception of what the good might itself be. The broad scope of such a question requires a framework that is equal to the task. Edwards's response is Beauty. Edwards makes the frequent suggestion that Beauty is "the central clue"[60] to the nature of reality. This idea of Beauty, as Delattre notes, is "primarily objective, structural, and relational rather than subjective, emotional, and relativist."[61] As we have seen, there is a relationship in Edwards's thought between the structure of reality itself (secondary beauty) and the structure of moral actions between sentient beings (primary beauty). In this way, he conceives goodness in his entire aesthetic vision for the universe. Moral goodness is understood as "cordial agreement or consent of being to being." [62] Here is where Edwards ventures his definition of true virtue. It most essentially consists in "benevolence to being in general."[63]

Thus, the good shepherd image of the pastor defines one of the primary initiatives of pastoral being in terms of a benevolence to being in general. This is another way of stating the importance of "being" a certain way in the world. The moral life is not a matter of following a list of regulations or even of interpreting the Bible in a certain way. It is a matter of facing the world with benevolence. It is a type of presence in the world. It is a purity of heart. Significantly, Jesus commends the pure in heart for their vision. He affirms that "they will see God" (Matt 5:8). His teaching here, embedded in the Sermon on the Mount, advocates a way of being over certain moral actions as the fundamental disposition of goodness. In his work on the virtues, Donald Capps suggests that the emphases of the Beatitudes of Jesus are powerful "because they encourage and undergird the dispositions that are fundamental to the saving virtues—engagement with the world, continuity and constancy,

---

60. Delattre, "Beauty and Theology," 85.
61. Ibid.
62. Edwards, *True Virtue*, 31.
63. Ibid., 3.

and vitality."⁶⁴ Thus, the "purity of heart" of the good shepherd is consonant with the whole moral vision propounded in the Beatitudes. As Capps notes, "The Beatitudes are not moral prescriptions or even ethical guidelines. They are an empathic endorsement of our longing for peace and well-being in the world and they reflect an unusually acute vision of how God even now is restoring the world."⁶⁵

I suggest that it is those who are "pure of heart" who already possess such a vision of how God is even now restoring the world. They will see God because, in a real sense, they have already seen God in his restorative acts in the created order. The good shepherd has an appreciation for the beauty of life, for the beauty in even that—especially that—which is, to others, disfigured, deficient, incomplete. The good shepherd assumes a posture in relation to others and to God that sees beauty and seeks ways to enable beauty to emerge from the shadows, giving it a chance to shine.

Love for God

A mature pastoral theology "is irreducibly religious and ethical."⁶⁶ As Hunter explains, this means that pastoral theology is concerned "first and finally with . . . the redemption of that which is lost and the fulfillment of that which is promised in and through the life and reality of God."⁶⁷ The pastor as good shepherd leans on his relationship with God as a fundamental posture in a broken world. The first and last response of the pastor as good shepherd is hope. The pastor has a sustained trust in the presence of One who is able to "make all things new." As Capps suggests, "The worldview that underlies the pastoral ministry is grounded in eternal hopefulness. To be a pastor means to be eternally hopeful."⁶⁸ Pastors who possess a mature pastoral theology of virtue are not unaware of the complex presence of evil and suffering. But despite these painful realities, or, rather, because of them, the pastor remains postured toward God in a disposition of hope. Hope, grounded in the reality of God who is "for us," may be thought of as the core "virtue" of the pastor.

---

64. Capps, *Deadly Sins and Saving Virtues*, 120.
65. Ibid., 135.
66. Hunter, "What Is Pastoral about Pastoral Theology," 45.
67. Ibid., 46.
68. Capps, *Agents of Hope*, 3.

I have followed Edwards in suggesting that an account of virtue without God is finally deficient. He insists that "true virtue must chiefly consist in love to God; the Being of beings, infinitely the greatest and best."[69] He is prepared to reject schemes of moral philosophy that do not give this supreme place to God, doing so not simply out of religious conviction, but out of a reasoned, thoughtful, yet decisive conception of the moral life. In his view, if love for God is not the "first and the last,"[70] a moral scheme, however otherwise sound, is deeply flawed. He writes:

> Hence it appears that those schemes of religion or moral philosophy, that—however well in some respects they may treat of benevolence to mankind and other virtues depending on it, yet—have not a supreme regard to God, and love to him laid as the foundation, and all other virtues handled in a connection with this, and in subordination to it, are not true schemes of philosophy, but are fundamentally and essentially defective.[71]

It is noteworthy that moral philosopher Alasdair MacIntyre has emphasized the importance of relating moral conceptions with a worldview that includes God.[72]

Though a full rendition of the dimensions of virtue is beyond the scope of this (and perhaps of any single) project, we may be convinced of the essential relationship virtue has to God. We may share Edwards's confidence that, whatever excellences or beauty virtue might have, it most certainly is derived from our relationship to God. In this light, the good shepherd weighs carefully the problem of theodicy. Suffering and the presence of evil are serious problems for the good shepherd. The presence of suffering and the human misery that accompanies the experiences of "forsakenness" threaten faith, and force one to the boundaries where absolute faith struggles with despair. Any theology (pastoral or otherwise) that does not enter into this abyss cannot suffice, for it would deny hope to the most vulnerable and forsaken.

---

69. Edwards, *True Virtue*, 4.
70. Ibid., 26.
71. Ibid.
72. MacIntyre, "Moral Philosophy," 14, states, "he makes clear what is also the plain implication of a number of other essays, that there is no sphere of morality independent of the agent's metaphysical or theological (or antitheological) view of the world and, more particularly, of God and the self."

Gutierrez suggests that this is the fundamental question about all theology: "Are suffering human beings able to enter into an authentic relationship with God and find a correct way of speaking about God?"[73] The good shepherd is less concerned, however, with speaking about God than he is about standing with those who have experienced themselves as forsaken by God. Moral vision is finally the capacity to enter into the suffering of others with the radical protest of hope. The good shepherd is prepared to lay down his life for the sheep. Can there be any greater or deeper consent to being than this? Perhaps here, in the ultimate consent to being through acceptance of non-being, moral philosophy, theology, and pastoral theology merge in the most complete sense. Somehow, in the mystery of God's active presence in a broken world, a shepherd dares to embrace the suffering of another in a willed act of solidarity that witnesses to an unshakeable hope in God. This is consent to being, the very epitome—and depth—of virtue.

A FINAL WORD

Rubem Alves has helped me in many ways to shake off the pre-formed ideas of theology that hinder my own feeble attempt to express the mystery of virtue. I close with a quotation from his book *What is Religion?* that expresses something of the on-going search that I am passionately called to share with other word-smiths and caregivers:

> The meaning of life is not a fact. In a world still under the sign of death, in which the highest values are crucified and brutality triumphs, it is an illusion to proclaim harmony with the universe as a present reality . . . God and the meaning of life are absences, realities for which we yearn, gifts of hope . . . As the trapeze artist must leap out over the abyss, abandoning every point of support, the religious soul also has to leap out over the abyss, toward the evidence of feelings, of the voice of love, of the suggestions of hope."[74]

In solidarity with all those who share a common vision for assisting the soul—especially the most anguished soul—toward suggestions of hope, I offer the glimpse of meaning that has come to mean most to me. Virtue means compassion: to suffer with.

Pati cum.

73. Gutierrez, *On Job*, 15.
74. Alves, *What Is Religion*, 90.

Appendix A

Key Events in the Life of Jonathan Edwards

1703   Jonathan Edwards born, October 5.
1716   Enters Yale College at 13 years of age.
1720   Graduates from Yale College and begins two years of graduate study.
1722   Edwards leaves for one year of ministry in New York.
1723   Edwards graduates with an MA from Yale College.
1724   Appointed tutor at Yale College and serves in this capacity until 1726 when he resigns and moves to Northampton.
1727   Ordained to the gospel Ministry, February 15.
             Married Sarah Pierrepont in New Haven in July.
1729   Solomon Stoddart, Edwards's maternal grandfather, dies. Edwards has been serving under Stoddart for three years, and continues to serve as Senior Minister for 21 further years.
1742   Visible Covenant drafted
1750   On June 22, 1750, the church Council recommends Edwards's dismissal. July 2, Edwards preaches his farewell sermon at Northampton.
1757   Named President of the College of New Jersey after seven years in Stockbridge, MA.
1758   Arrives in Princeton, February, 1758.
             Dies March 22, 1758, at age 54.

Appendix B

Significant Writings of Jonathan Edwards

1719	*Notes on the Mind*, Senior at Yale College, 72 entries
1722–26	Begins *Diary*, December 19, 1722
1724	*Resolutions*
1731	*God Glorified in Man's Dependence*
1734	*A Divine and Supernatural Light Imparted on the Soul by the Spirit of God*
1737	*A Faithful Narrative of the Surprising Works of God*
1738	*Charity and Its Fruits*; *Discourses on Various Important Subjects*
1739–40	*Personal Narrative of Jonathan Edwards*
1741	*Distinguishing Marks of a Work of the Spirit*; *Sinners in the Hands of an Angry God*
1743	*Some Thoughts on Revival*
1744	*True Excellency of a Gospel Minister*
1746	*Treatise on Religious Affections*
1747	*True Saints, When Absent from the Body, Are Present with the Lord*; *An Humble Attempt to Promote Explicit Agreement*
1749	*The Life and Diary of David Brainerd*; *Concerning Qualifications for Full Communion*
1750	*A Farewell Sermon to the People of Northampton*
1753	*True Grace Distinguished from the Experience of Devils*
1753–54	*Dissertation concerning the End of Creation*
1754	*On the Freedom of the Will*
1755	*The Nature of True Virtue*

Appendix C

The Seven Days of Virtue

At the heart of the enterprise of pastoral theology is the significant confluence of suffering and hope. In this book I argue for the idea that a pastoral theology of virtue demands a co-participation in the experiences of suffering that can be articulated in parabolic word-forms. I pointed to the use of autobiography as an important signal to authentic pastoral action. While moral vision will demand more than the imaginative use of language, I have argued for an ontological idea of consent to being as a unique construct of virtue as compassion. The autobiographical piece offered in this appendix is my own attempt to articulate the quest for solidarity in my own efforts as a person and as a pastor. I offer it with the sincere hope that it will inspire further creative reflection on the source of moral vision and the ways in which we might continue to stay near to those who suffer as a fundamental posture of consent to being in a broken world.

THE SEVEN DAYS OF VIRTUE

Captured by the importance of his pursuit of the Good, the word-smith calculated every twist in the plot, every turn of the phrase, each placement of a word. The words must be true. The words must speak the truth about virtue. The words must reflect something deeper to which they point. Goodness must prevail.

Life was fragrant and good and the word-smith enjoyed his work. He hammered and forged new items each week that he would bring to the market. He particularly enjoyed the market. It was the one chance each week to break away from the hard work of the word shop and to share the wares with those who came to listen. At the market laughter and deception lived together. It was the most interesting place to take words. One never knew quite what to expect.

Many persons came shopping at the market. Young and old would gather each week—almost ritually. Some had long since quit word-shopping; others were sincerely looking for a new word. Like Maria. She was a young and vibrant business woman. They say that it was common knowledge that her marriage was "in trouble." Words buzzed around and (mostly) behind her. They said something about fault, something about the children. Cruelty was mentioned. Maria would ignore these words. She came because the word-smith had something prepared and she wanted to see if it could mean anything to her. She listened as the word-smith spun his stories. Something about grace. Something about making it through. Something about what Maria longed to hear most—that Someone loved her.

The word-smith thought diligently about those who might come to the market each week. He thought about Maria. He considered the others: the widower who longed for some companion-word. The lonely who longed for a word-friend. The blind lady who wanted words that could allow her to see. He thought about all of these and the many others who might come to the market.

The word-critics would come too! Oh, they would never miss! No siree! Often they would come and steal words without paying for them. It bothered the word-smith, especially if they took words that others needed. The market was filled with laughter and deception. Days and weeks and months passed. Few things changed at the word market. At least so it appeared.

Then a terrible thing happened! It was unexpected and quite alarming. The word-smith was injured on the job. He had been carrying on his usual routine and something happened. The words began to seem hidden to him. He would look in the same ways and in the same places—but the meanings were gone. It was quite unnerving for him.

He tried to combat the problem by redoubling his efforts. The harder he tried, the more painful each day became at the word shop. The stories would seem wordless. The phrases and synonyms that he used to count on would hide. Verses seemed distorted and changed. Something terrible had gone wrong!

What was worse was that the market was no longer any fun. The people had stopped laughing; deception grew bolder and became scorn.

The market still came and went every week but the word-smith had so little to sell. He knew he wouldn't be able to survive long on the few words that he was selling. His despondency deepened. Words became heavy and felt like giant boulders as he attempted to drag them around the word-shop. It all became quite difficult and the word-smith knew he would have to make changes.

So, after eleven years at his craft the word-smith swept out the few remaining phrases and words left lying around the word-shop and he stopped giving out any words. He knew that he needed to find the meanings again. There had to be some way that he could recapture the joy that the words brought him. He shut out the lights and closed the shop door—thinking that somehow he would be back. He sold many of his word-smith tools. The others he packed away for another day.

The word-smith applied for a job at a health clinic. The health clinic was a totally different experience for the word-smith. He often felt out of place. People didn't care much about his phrases there. They seldom said much of anything. The people at the health clinic didn't say much because most of them were sick and needed help. Wounds were bandaged to keep them from bleeding or getting infected. Common medicines were dispensed freely. Sometimes it was simply a nutrition supplement or some fluids for those who had become dehydrated. The health clinic was a busy place of few words.

The word-smith soon caught on. It was not long before he was right in there dispensing pills, fixing up the clinic, and helping to bandage wounds. He found the work refreshing and often lost himself in the tasks at the clinic. The work was strenuous but meaningful. It was a good feeling to see wounds bandaged and to experience the many needs of the sick being met each day.

Some nights he would go home and ponder the words that he used to sell at the market. Occasionally he would think of a new meaning, something that had never occurred to him before his experiences at the health clinic. Once in a while he would even drive by the old word shop to see if other word-smiths were working there. They were. He wondered if the words he used to sell still had meaning for Maria and the others who had come. He wondered what the new word-smiths were crafting and how those meanings were being received at the market.

These reflections gave him reason to consider. What if the meanings could be restored? What if the injury he had suffered was simply the catalyst to allow him to come to the clinic—to see new meanings? Something powerful began to emerge as he pondered these possibilities.

A Wind passed through. Its source was imperceptible. Its course was unknown. The wind blew for seven days and seven nights: at times whispering, at times gusting into a fierce gale.

The word-smith noted the days in his journal:

"Virtue. What is it?" he wrote. "Could it be a sham? A religious game of gaining brownie points with God? The good do what is right and are blessed? The wicked reap what they sow? Life is fair?

"Not a chance.

"Not a chance or a prayer.

"The reality must be deeper. I must descend into the abyss and find the words. The words I used to know so well like hope, joy, strength, and so many others. They are all in the abyss—the place of hidden words. The abyss itself is clouded with mist, surrounded by silence. I must risk entering the great abyss. I know virtue is down there—I sense it.

"I do not mind confessing to you that I am afraid. I know the power that words have. They can kill. I have seen words rip the soul out of a strong man and, weakened by the absence of a retort, he took his own life. I have seen words heal and I have seen words destroy. I know that going into the void will be dangerous. I would be crazy if I told you I had no fear. One word has more power than entire worlds and universes. I would be lying if I told you I was not afraid. I am afraid.

"Still, the abyss beckons. I must go. It seems like a destiny. Down there I know I will find virtue. I must. It is the word that I have been trying to write my whole life. Its meaning is the meaning I have been searching for all of these years in word school.

"When I was injured—that's when I knew that I would go to the abyss. I was left with no choice. The old phrases and words have no power. Not with the injury.

"And that's not the only reason I am going. My work at the clinic has reminded me that there are so many injuries. So many painful memories. The words are for all of us —the injured, the wounded, the broken lives. I have seen so much and I am so young. Take note of my journal. It has seven days. On the seventh day I will return with virtue.

Day One: Pretend

It's so dark down here. I am learning to cope with the terror of the Absence of light. Monitoring my own response I notice that fear pervades my being. I am afraid, groping. Fear crawls on my skin.

And so I must pretend. I pretend that there is light. That all is well. That I'm just like the others back at the market. I pretend that it is not this dark. I pretend that fear is a friend. That my hope is real.

You remember that word don't you?

> Pretend:
> inauthentic, not for real, false front, hiding something, masking, deceit, self-deception, afraid to tell, prone to avoid the truth, "don't want to be a burden"

This dark and lonely first day profoundly grips my soul. Everything is difficult. I try to remember the days at the market. The days in the light. I try to feel unafraid. To cope better.

Why did I come here? I sense that I am angry but I don't know why. Why?

Why am I down here? Why did no one else come? Did I have to come alone? Why am I crying? Did the sun become black?

It is frightening down here in pretence.

I have never been shrouded in the Darkness before. I am aware of great fears. I hear the words and the sounds that deepen my fear:

I hear a mother scream, "My baby is dead! My baby is dead!" And a brother weeps at his grievous sin—he killed his brother. A wife died and I can hear the husband putting on his mask of words, "At least she didn't suffer long." The mask wills to hide the painful truth. It decides to protect the brokenness from view. It shapes reality into its mould. It wills—Pretense.

The first day is forever.
It is pitch black down here.
I cringe in the darkness and hide.
Pretend
Pretend it's a normal meal.
That nothing is different.
Ask for the normal ...
Thousand Island please.
And ignore.

The thing that disturbs.
The thing that frightens and comforts.
The thing that makes you different.
Where others stare.
Pretend you're o.k.
Hide your fear
Bury your agonies . . . one by one.
Run to the gallery and buy a mask.
And don't forget to wear it.
Be hidden. Hide away in fear.
And when you can't hide . . .
Pretend in fear.
Pretend you're the same.
Pretend it doesn't matter.
Pretend you don't need to change.
Pretend your life isn't unique.
Night falls deep.

Day Two: The Source

It's early in the day and there is a simple light—like the light of dawn sustained for hours. It is subdued but the shadows can be made out. The mask leaks in some light.

There!

In the bush . . . did you see it?

Hope . . . it was a hope? Or was it a wish?

If it was a hope I can tell you what it was like. There's no mistaking a hope for a wish. A wish is still and lifeless like a portrait. It has the appearance of a hope but it doesn't move. It must be moved. Wishes are given and taken. They are purchased and exchanged. Received and spent. They have no life of their own. Interesting but life-less.

Hopes are alive! They bound . . . they streak across the dim sky and flash something real; something alive!

Hopes always return to the Source. All hopes come from the Source and return to the Source. Sometimes they are simply mists against the streams of sunlight—forming a rainbow—the Sign. Other times they are almost tangible—you feel like you could reach out and embrace them. When you try you discover that they are far off—it's an illusion that they are near.

Day two is pleasant. The darkness still oppresses but those hopes! They really are remarkable. I could sit here for hours just watching them. Drinking in the rainbows! Oh, the rainbows!

There are undefined moments when it seems like the rainbows are formed through my tears. Like the mist is from me and the clarity of the hope is fractured into a thousand blends of color. Perhaps that is real. I cannot tell from this vantage point.

I have decided to make this a long day. I want to stay here a while. I want to study the hopes to see where they lead. I want to go to the Source. It is clear to me that the hopes cannot be embraced in themselves. Perhaps if I could follow them to the source?

What a miracle this day is. Nothing seems real.

What a mystery this day has become. I am more awake than ever before and the endless sight of rainbows against the dim sky is unthinkable. I wish Maria were here. She would love this. And the others from the market.

The night of darkness is past. Hopes abound.

Did You See It?

... did you see it?

... a flash ... a light—bounding past ...

... so small, but real ... a hope.

... can you tell where it is going?

... the bouncing truth ...

so imperceptible ... but real ...

a direction to follow ... unseen hope.

... will you trust its promise?

... to guide your lives?

... to honor your faith?

... to lead you to the Source?

... have you seen the rainbows?

... through the mists

of your broken dreams? ...

... will you rest ...

and stay ...

... past hope?

Night falls lightly.

Day Three: Affliction's Desert

This morning I crossed the source of hope. I sense the hard part of the journey at hand. I am being led into the desert. The reputation of the desert is fierce. The enemy is there. Some say it is Dread. The reputation is Affliction.

Those who know something have told me that the darkness was only a prelude to today. I am told that Affliction will try to kill me. That he will capture me and torture me—burning my flesh while keeping me alive in a trap. They tell me that Affliction drinks the hopes of its victims. If it can. It feeds on the flesh of the hopeful.

Lord, strengthen me.

I remember the words you told us to say:

Our Father in heaven,

Hallowed be your name,

your kingdom come,

your will be done on earth as it is in heaven.

Give us today our daily bread.

Forgive us our debts,

as we have also forgiven our debtors.

And lead us not into temptation,

but deliver us from the evil one.

Strange.

I led the people at the market with these words so many times. We sang them. We loved them. We ate these words. Until today I don't think I really knew what they meant or why you told us to say them. I am so ashamed of myself!

It is

evening now.

Affliction has come to confront me. I feel forgotten—no, forsaken. The memories I have right now are severe:

The mother stands weeping at the graveside of her daughter. I hear her anguished cry, "Why not me? Why her? She was so young."

. . . a sister is killed in a head on collision.

. . . a husband's leg is torn off in an industrial accident.

. . . a son's life is snuffed out by a motorcycle sliding on the wet pavement.

. . . a father dies—cancer.

...a malignant brain tumor takes a beautiful, bright young mother—the girls she leaves behind don't even know how to cry

...mental illness

...suicide

...sexual abuse

Affliction torments me with these painful memories. And, when I struggle for hope, the scorpion's sting is inflicted. Words I never thought I would hear:

"Your daughter has a lesion on her spine. She will be irreversibly disabled from the waist down. She will have many things taken from her and you will have to teach her to compensate. She will be broken and you will not be able to fix her. She will suffer many things, and you will watch. All of the suffering of the world will seem like nothing as you stand by and watch your baby endure pain. You will see your wife broken into pieces and your world will crumble around you. This is your affliction."

He laughs and leaves.

Affliction

Give me death.

I cannot stand. My knees falter

as I anticipate her pain.

Give me death.

I dread the truth; the stinking

reality...its doom and persistent stab.

Hurt...

Give me death.

The

trust is broken. I cannot

see...why?

All sorrow...and we suffer.

Give me death.

This enemy wants to torture me.

I will not make it.

Help.

Dread is come.

It fills all spaces...

hopes are dashed.

Forsaken, I sink.

Night.

Day Four: The Dream

I cried for a thousand years last night. Not only for my affliction but for the afflictions of so many. For Maria and the others. For unnamed mothers and fathers who buried their children. For the thousands of little ones. Somehow, in my affliction there came a solidarity with those who suffer. An understanding. A comprehension.

My tears flowed without stopping until, exhausted, I fell on the hard desert ground. While I was sleeping I had a dream.

In my dream I was not a broken father or a word-smith or a worker at the clinic.

I was a son. My Father came to me with a tenderness and a compassion that dwarfed anything I had ever known. Like an artist approaches a new canvas.

The servants were the first ones to see me lying on the ground and they went to get supplies to make me comfortable. While they were gone my father came himself and put his coat around me and carried me like he had when I was a child. He carried me back to the house and, as he carried me he wept. His tears were not for himself—they were for me. He knew that life would wound me and he understood my affliction. Those tears meant everything to me! I knew for the first time in my life that I was safe.

When we got to the house he told me about his own afflictions. This tragedy in my life had changed everything. It was as if I never knew him before. He was telling me things I had no idea about. He told me the secret things about the betrayal and brokenness and death's sting. He used all my favorite words as he spoke and he told me what they meant. Before I woke I asked him, "What is virtue?"

He told me.
VISION
up . . .
raised up . . .
raised up above . . .
raised up above fear.
up . . .
to the sacred hope . . .
with love filled and laughter growing.
And the Sacred
sings a bright, new song!

up ...
beyond anguish or sin ...
free ...
Grace.
up ...
to newness and spring
and gladness forgotten.
up ...
didn't our hearts burn? when he spoke?
... and when he broke the bread ...
... didn't we see him?
... and didn't he sing?
"Behold I am making all things new."

It's morning now and as I awake from my dream I become aware of a new horizon. Where I was in the desert made it impossible for me to see last night and besides, think of my emotional state. How could I have seen anything?

Awakened by the morning sun I look out and there is a field of what seem like flowers. My search is over. It is a field of words and their meanings. The ones my father told me about in the dream. They are all here ... and they're real.

I know what I must do today.

I must pick the words and carefully arrange them in order. I will be a word designer and I will make a fragrant bouquet. It will mean attention to every detail of art, beauty, and design that I have ever known or imagined. It will require that I remember the words he told me in the dream and see their meanings. And, if I am successful, let me declare it to you now—I will name the fragrant bouquet "virtue" and I will tell you the meanings that he gave to me in the dream:

Courage—the ability to stand in the face of impending danger without fear

Hope—the sense of promise behind the brokenness in our lives

Trust—living in the confidence of the unseen

Love—the perfect expression of God's character repeated in our life

Affliction—a moment without God

Suffering—agonizing separation from the comfort of God

Peace—an abiding sense of God's presence

Grace—the touch of God
Gratitude—the disposition of one touched by God
Faith—the way through
Forgiveness—the exchange of good for evil
Friendship—loyalty to the well-being of another
Freedom—embracing the infinite
Honor—God's blessing
Contentment—resting in God's goodness
Goodness—the creativity of God
Compassion—to suffer with
Integrity—agreement of mind, will, and heart

These are most of the words I can remember. They all have a part in the fragrant bouquet. I must admit to you that I feel inadequate to be a word designer. I am a simple word-smith by trade really. Word designers always amaze me. They seem to know just where to place the words.

What could a simple father know about designing words? How could the suffering of my little child make a difference in the world where words have meaning? As a word-smith, a father, and a worker in the clinic, my talents seem completely inadequate for the task.

On the other hand, I did have the dream. And besides, I have seen the field of words and their meanings and it is real. It was my father who told me the meanings and when I asked him, "What is virtue?" he did tell me.

So, even though it may seem foolish to other word designers, I must tell you now the meaning that he gave me. He told me that "virtue is consent to Being."

Day Five: Walking with the Wounded

My vision is clear as I leave the field and return to the familiar places of the clinic and the market. I have a new sense of mission and destiny. Everything is in its rightful place.

"The one who walked in darkness has seen a great light …"

"The people who walked in darkness have seen a great light …"

What is clear to me is the calling to serve others. To help. To meet needs. To testify about the dream. To declare:

Easter.

Day.

Life

"Who will separate us from the love of God?"
"I know that my Redeemer lives."

My wounds are healed. The wounded now becomes a healer. The broken are sought out. A new purpose ... ministry.

To serve those who are broken. To give life to those who are dying. To hold and comfort the afflicted in their pain. To break the stronghold of the oppressors and set the captives free. To proclaim the Jubilee. To sing the song of freedom.

  ... a wounded soldier tells a battle story and in his speaking a scar is healed.

  ... a homeless woman finds a bed and a meal prepared for her with tender hands ... it's not a home yet, but oh, the healing of a good meal and a warm place to rest ... and love.

  ... a teenager is held—maybe for the first time by a caring adult.

  ... a child is rescued from the street.

  ... a bowl of soup and a sweater leave the suburbs in a Suburban and make their way to the inner city.

  ... a friendless convict learns the name of a person who wants to be his friend.

Ministry. Forgiveness is offered and accepted. Tears are shared. Burdens are shouldered. Dreams are encouraged. Courage grows. Love deepens. Sacrifices seem easy. Scorn shrinks low.

MINISTRY
  ... can I have this mattress?
  ... any clothes for my nakedness?
  ... can you spare some change?
  ... mind if I die here?
  ... here, take my coat.
  ... do you have a place to stay?
  ... finish caring for him and I will pay you when I return.
  ... she will not die alone.
  ... Aha.

Now I see ... to do this kindness matters.
Now ... to stop the silent crying ...
Now ... my care to express ...
Now ... I hear ... His calling voice,
  ... can I have this mattress?
  ... any clothes for my nakedness?

... can you spare some change?
... mind if I live here?

Day Six: We Stand Together

Life is getting better for me.

Meaning.

The reality is that there is more solidarity in suffering that I ever dreamed as a word-smith. "A cord of three strands is not easily broken." There is a sense of belonging that I never had before at the market or the clinic.

What is new?

I am new.

I am converted.

I am transformed.

Most wouldn't say that there is much different. I still use the words. I still do things associated with the clinic. So, what is different?

Solidarity. A sense that what I am doing matters not just to me but to many. "He who saves one life saves the world entire."

Connections are made that were missing before. Words connect with actions and actions connect with words. The market moves into the clinic. Amazing.

There is a whole new sense of where this is leading. It is not alone or even a small group. All of us—together—join hands and hearts and wills.

The kingdom is at hand.

"Your will be done on earth as it is in heaven."

The virtues are not meant for one but for all.

One heals, we all live.

One hurts, we all suffer.

One dies, we all grieve.

One gives, we all benefit. One helps, we all become kinder. Community and care are knit together. We are not alone in our afflictions.

Virtue grows up and becomes a community.

Together

Touched by your kindness, the world gets brighter.

Our hopes collide and grow side by side.

Faith and works cultivate the land ...

for a better neighborhood.

Binding love strengthens cords to infinity.
Laughter swells.
Fear takes flight...
and, laughing, we pursue.
We ache with laughter as we run.
Creative.
We share our gifts.
We work in harmony...
Towards a common destiny...for all.
Called by One who cares most deeply.
Tapestry of virtues.
Treasured memories.
Binding love.
What would we do without each other?

Day Seven: On the Seventh Day

I have always known that one day I would stop striving. That I would give up my competitive ways and rest. I knew, somehow, that there would come a time when my work was not required. When all work became obsolete.

That day has come.

My only surprise is that it has come now. I expected it to be far away in the distant future. I anticipated a retirement in the golden years.

Go figure.

There is something incredibly constructive in this rest. I am finding that most of the things that need doing can be done without my skills, or talents, or even the words.

Deeds flow out of the community we have built.

Words speak for themselves.

The words and deeds have their own will and their own power.

We rest.

The nice part of rest is the glory of seeing "all things being made new."

When you're so busy, you miss it all.

The child's smile. The sunset on the river. The laughter in the halls.

There are so many beautiful sights, sounds, smells, and tastes.

The tapestry of life is now complete.

Creative work...stops.

We're home.
Consent to Being.
REST
I don't know if I really believed this day would come.
The chapel is prepared.
The bride of unsurpassed beauty arrives.
She is stunning.
I can't believe we're here.
At the altar.
Taking each other.
Fulfilled longing.
Forgotten sorrow.
I remember this place.
I have been here before.
Love's beauty repeated.
 . . . that moment.
 . . . that lifetime.
Infinity.
Agreed.

Bibliography

Alderman, Harold. "By Virtue of a Virtue." In *Virtue Ethics: A Critical Reader*, edited by Daniel Statman, 143–65. Washington, DC: Georgetown University Press, 1997.
Alves, Rubem A. *The Poet, The Warrior, The Prophet*. London: SCM; Philadelphia, PA: Trinity Press International, 1990.
———. *What is Religion?* Maryknoll, NY: Orbis, 1984.
Aristotle. *The Nicomachean Ethics*. Translated by J. A. K. Thomson. New York: Penguin, 1976.
Berger, Peter L. *The Sacred Canopy: Elements of a Sociological Theory of Religion*. New York and Toronto: Doubleday, 1967.
Boisen, Anton. "The Distinctive Task of the Minister." *Pastoral Psychology* 2 (1952) 10–15.
Bonhoeffer, Dietrich. *Ethics*. New York: Macmillan, 1955.
———. *Letters and Papers from Prison*. Enlarged ed. New York: Macmillan, 1972.
Brockelman, Paul T. *Existential Phenomenology and the World of Ordinary Experience: An Introduction*. Washington, DC: University Press of America, 1980.
Browning, Don S. *The Moral Context of Pastoral Care*. Philadelphia: Westminster, 1976.
———. "Pastoral Theology in a Pluralistic Age." *Pastoral Psychology* 29 (1980) 24–35.
Brueggemann, Walter. *Finally Comes the Poet: Daring Speech for Proclamation*. Minneapolis: Fortress, 1989.
Burck, J. R., and Rodney J. Hunter. "Protestant Pastoral Theology." In *Dictionary of Pastoral Care and Counseling*. Edited by Rodney J. Hunter, 867–72. Nashville: Abingdon, 1990.
Byrnes, Thomas A. "H. Richard Niebuhr's Reconstruction of Jonathan Edwards' Moral Theology." In *The Annual of the Society of Christian Ethics 1985*, edited by Alan B. Anderson, 33–56. Washington, DC: The Society of Christian Ethics, 1986.
Campbell, Alastair V. *Rediscovering Pastoral Care*. Philadelphia: Westminster, 1981.
Capps, Donald. *Agents of Hope: A Pastoral Psychology*. Minneapolis: Fortress, 1995.
———. *Biblical Approaches to Pastoral Counseling*. Philadelphia: Westminster, 1981.
———. *The Child's Song: The Religious Abuse of Children*. Louisville: Westminster John Knox, 1995.
———. *Deadly Sins and Saving Virtues*. Philadelphia: Fortress, 1987.
———. *Pastoral Care and Hermeneutics*. Philadelphia: Westminster, 1984.
———. *The Poet's Gift: Toward the Renewal of Pastoral Care*. Louisville: Westminster John Knox, 1993.
———. *Reframing: A New Method in Pastoral Care*. Minneapolis: Fortress, 1990.
Cessario, Romanus. *The Moral Virtues and Theological Ethics*. Notre Dame, IN: University of Notre Dame, 1991.
Cone, James. *God of the Oppressed*. New York: Seabury, 1975.

Conly, Sarah. "Flourishing and the Ethics of Virtue." In *Midwest Studies in Philosophy*. XIII. *Ethical Theory: Character and Virtue*, edited by Peter A. French, Theodore E. Uehling, and Howard K. Wettstein, 83–96. Notre Dame, IN: University of Notre Dame, 1988.

Delattre, Roland Andre. *Beauty and Sensibility in the Thought of Jonathan Edwards: An Essay in Aesthetics and Theological Ethics*. New Haven: Yale University Press, 1969.

———. "Beauty and Theology: A Reappraisal of Jonathan Edwards." In *Critical Essays on Jonathan Edwards*, edited by William J. Scheick, 136–50. Boston: Hall, 1980.

———. "The Theological Ethics of Jonathan Edwards: An Homage to Paul Ramsey." *The Journal of Religious Ethics* 19 (1991) 71–102.

Dwight, Sereno E., ed. *The Works of Jonathan Edwards*. 2 vols. Revised and corrected by Edward Hickman (1834). Reprint, Carlisle, PA: Banner of Truth, 1974.

Edwards, Jonathan. "A Faithful Narrative of the Surprising Work of God." In Dwight, ed., *The Works of Jonathan Edwards*, 1:344–46.

———. "A Farewell Sermon." In Dwight, ed., *The Works of Jonathan Edwards*, 1:cxcvii–ccvii.

———. "God Glorified in Man's Dependence." In Dwight, ed., *The Works of Jonathan Edwards*, 2:3–7.

———. "An Humble Inquiry into the Rules of the Word of God concerning the Qualifications Requisite to a Complete Standing and Full Communion in the Visible Christian Church." In Dwight, ed., *The Works of Jonathan Edwards*, 1:431–84.

———. "Justification by Faith Alone." In Dwight, ed., *The Works of Jonathan Edwards*, 1:622-24.

———. "Memoirs of Jonathan Edwards, A.M." In Dwight, ed., *The Works of Jonathan Edwards*, 1:xi–ccxxxiv. (Includes the Memoirs and an Appendix)

———. *The Nature of True Virtue*. 1765. Reprint, Ann Arbor, MI: The University of Michigan Press, 1960.

———. "On the Freedom of the Will." In Dwight, ed., *The Works of Jonathan Edwards*, 1:3–93.

———. *The Religious Affections*. 1746. Reprint, Carlisle, PA: Banner of Truth, 1986.

———. "Sinners in the Hands of an Angry God." In Dwight, ed., *The Works of Jonathan Edwards*, 2:7–12.

———. "The True Excellency of a Gospel Minister." In Dwight, ed., *The Works of Jonathan Edwards*, 2:955–60.

Erikson, Joan M. *Wisdom and the Senses: The Way of Creativity*. New York: Norton, 1988.

Farley, Benjamin W. *In Praise of Virtue: An Exploration of the Biblical Virtues in a Christian Context*. Grand Rapids: Eerdmans, 1995.

Fiddes, Paul S. *The Creative Suffering of God*. Oxford: Oxford University Press, 1988.

Ford, S. Dennis. *Sins of Omission: A Primer on Moral Indifference*. Minneapolis: Fortress, 1990.

Gilligan, Carol. *In a Different Voice: Psychological Theory and Women's Development*. Cambridge, MA: Harvard University Press, 1982.

Gutierrez, Gustavo. *On Job: God-Talk and the Suffering of the Innocent*. Maryknoll, NY: Orbis, 1987.

Haring, Bernard. *The Virtues of an Authentic Life: A Celebration of Spiritual Maturity*. Translated by Peter Heinegg. Ligouri, MO: Ligouri, 1997.

Bibliography

Holbrook, Clyde A. *The Ethics of Jonathan Edwards*. Ann Arbor, MI: University of Michigan Press, 1973.

Hulme, William E. *Pastoral Care and Counseling: Using the Unique Resources of the Christian Tradition*. Minneapolis: Augsburg, 1981.

Hunter, Rodney J. "The Future of Pastoral Theology." *Pastoral Psychology* 29 (1980) 58–69.

———. "What Is Pastoral about Pastoral Theology? Insights from Eight Years Shepherding the Dictionary of Pastoral Care and Counseling." *Journal of Pastoral Theology* 1 (1991) 35–52.

Hunter, Rodney J., and John Patton. "The Therapeutic Tradition's Theological and Ethical Commitments Viewed through Its Pedagogical Practices: A Tradition in Transition." In *Pastoral Care and Social Conflict*, edited by Pamela D. Couture and Rodney J. Hunter, 32–43. Nashville: Abingdon, 1995.

Jennings, T. W. Jr. "Pastoral Theological Methodology." In *Dictionary of Pastoral Care and Counseling*, edited by Rodney J. Hunter, 862–64. Nashville: Abingdon, 1990.

Jones, David Carlisle. *Biblical Christian Ethics*. Grand Rapids: Baker, 1994.

Kotva, Joseph J. *The Christian Case for Virtue Ethics*. Washington, DC: Georgetown University Press, 1996.

Kreeft, Peter. *Back to Virtue*. San Francisco: Ignatius, 1992.

———. *Making Sense out of Suffering*. Ann Arbor, MI: Servant Books, 1986.

Langan, John P. "Augustine on the Unity and the Interconnection of the Virtues." *Harvard Theological Review* 72 (1979) 81–95.

Lee, Sang Hyan. *The Philosophical Theology of Jonathan Edwards*. Princeton, NJ: Princeton University Press, 1988.

Levan, Christopher. *God Hates Religion: How the Gospels Condemn False Religious Practice*. Etobicoke, ON: United Church Press, 1995.

Loder, James E. *The Transforming Moment: Understanding Convictional Experiences*. San Francisco: Harper & Row, 1981.

MacIntyre, Alasdair. *After Virtue: A Study in Moral Theory*. Notre Dame, IN: University of Notre Dame Press, 1984.

———. "Moral Philosophy: What Next?" In *Revisions: Changing Perspectives in Moral Philosophy*, by Alasdair MacIntyre and Stanley Hauerwas, 1–15. Notre Dame, IN: University of Notre Dame Press, 1983.

Meilaender, Gilbert C. *The Theory and Practice of Virtue*. Notre Dame, IN: University of Notre Dame Press, 1984.

Merleau-Ponty, Maurice. *Phenomenology of Perception*. London: Routledge & Kegan Paul, 1972.

Miller, Perry. "Edwards, Locke, and the Rhetoric of Sensation." In *Critical Essays on Jonathan Edwards*, edited by William Scheick, 120–35. Boston: Hall, 1980.

Moltmann, Jurgen. *The Crucified God*. Philadelphia: SCM, 1974.

———. *Experiences of God*. Philadelphia: Fortress, 1980.

———. *Theology of Hope*. New York: Harper & Row, 1967. Reprint, San Francisco: Harper & Row, 1991.

Murdoch, Iris. *The Sovereignty of Good*. London: Routledge & Kegan Paul, 1970.

Murray, Iain H. *Jonathan Edwards: A New Biography*. Edinburgh and Carlisle, PA: Banner of Truth, 1987.

Niebuhr, H. Richard. *The Responsible Self: An Essay on Christian Moral Philosophy*. Library of Theological Ethics. Louisville: Westminster John Knox, 1999.

Nouwen, Henri J. M. *The Wounded Healer*. New York: Image Books, Doubleday, 1972.

Patton, John. *From Ministry to Theology: Pastoral Action and Reflection*. Nashville: Abingdon, 1990.

Peterson, Eugene H. *Under the Unpredictable Plant: An Exploration in Vocational Holiness*. Grand Rapids: Eerdmans, 1992.

Proudfoot, Wayne. "From Theology to a Science of Religions: Jonathan Edwards and William James on Religious Affections." *Harvard Theological Review* 82 (1989) 149-68.

Ramsey, Paul. "Jonathan Edwards and the Splendor of Common Morality." *This World* 25 (Spring 1989) 5-25.

Ramsey, Paul, ed. *Jonathan Edwards: Ethical Writings*. The Works of Jonathan Edwards 8. New Haven: Yale University Press, 1989.

Rilke, Rainer Maria. *Letters to a Young Poet*. Translated by M. D. H. Norton. 1934. Reprint, New York: Norton, 1962.

Rogers, Carl. *On Becoming a Person*. Boston: Houghton Mifflin, 1961.

Romero, Oscar. "Creating the Church of Tomorrow." *Brothers of Shepherd's Staff: Newsletter of Brothers of the Good Shepherd* (Fall 2008) 7. On-line: http://www.lbgs.org/ss/Fall%202008%20Newsletter.pdf.

Rorty, Amelie O. "Virtues and Their Vicissitudes." In *Midwest Studies in Philosophy*. XIII. *Ethical Theory: Character and Virtue*, edited by Peter A. French, Theodore E. Uehling, and Howard K. Wettstein, 136-48. Notre Dame, IN: University of Notre Dame Press, 1988.

Simonson, Harold P. *Jonathan Edwards: Theologian of the Heart*. Grand Rapids: Eerdmans, 1974.

Soelle, Dorothee. *Suffering*. Translated by Everett R. Kalin. Philadelphia: Fortress, 1975.

Solomon, David. "Internal Objections to Virtue Ethics." In *Midwest Studies in Philosophy*. XIII. *Ethical Theory: Character and Virtue*, edited by Peter A. French, Theodore E. Uehling, and Howard K. Wettstein, 428-41. Notre Dame, IN: University of Notre Dame Press, 1988.

Statman, Daniel. *Virtue Ethics: A Critical Reader*. Washington, DC: Georgetown University Press, 1997.

SteinhoffSmith, Roy. "The Politics of Pastoral Care: An Alternative Politics of Care." In *Pastoral Care and Social Conflict*. Edited by Pamela D. Couture and Rodney J. Hunter, 141-51. Nashville: Abingdon, 1995.

Stone, Bryan P. *Compassionate Ministry: Theological Foundations*. Maryknoll, NY: Orbis, 1996.

Tillich, Paul. *Biblical Religion and the Search for Ultimate Reality*. Chicago: University of Chicago Press, 1955.

———. *The Courage to Be*. Glasgow: Collins, 1952.

———. *Theology of Culture*. New York: Oxford University Press, 1959.

Wallace, James D. "Ethics and the Craft Analogy." In *Midwest Studies in Philosophy*. XIII. *Ethical Theory: Character and Virtue*, edited by Peter A. French, Theodore E. Uehling, and Howard K. Wettstein, 222-32. Notre Dame, IN: University of Notre Dame Press, 1988.

Watzlawick, Paul, John Weakland, and Richard Fisch. *Change: Principles of Problem Formation and Problem Resolution*. New York: Norton, 1974.

Weil, Simone. *Gravity and Grace*. 1952. Reprint, London: Routledge & Kegan Paul, 1963.

Westra, Helen Petter. "'Above All Others': Jonathan Edwards and the Gospel Ministry." *American Presbyterians* 67 (1989) 209–19.
Whitehead, Alfred North. *Religion in the Making.* New York: Meridian, 1960.
Wilcox, Mary W. *Developmental Journey.* Nashville: Abingdon, 1979.
Winslow, Ola. *Jonathan Edwards 1703–1758.* New York: Collier, 1961.

Suggestions for Further Reading

Alves, Rubem A. *Protestantism and Repression: A Brazilian Case Study.* Maryknoll, NY: Orbis, 1985.

———. *A Theology of Human Hope.* Washington, DC: Corpus, 1969.

———. *Tomorrow's Child: Imagination, Creativity and the Rebirth of Culture.* New York: Harper & Row, 1972.

Barbour, John D. *Tragedy as a Critique of Virtue.* Chico, CA: Scholars, 1984.

Beker, J. Christiaan. *Suffering and Hope: The Biblical Vision and the Human Predicament.* Philadelphia: Fortress, 1987. Reprint, Grand Rapids: Eerdmans, 1994.

Bonhoeffer, Dietrich. *Life Together.* San Francisco: Harper & Row, 1954.

Browning, Don S. *A Fundamental Practical Theology: Descriptive and Strategic Proposals.* Minneapolis: Fortress, 1991.

———. "The Pastoral Counselor as Ethicist: What Difference Do We Make?" *Journal of Pastoral Care* 42 (1988) 283–96.

———. *Religious Ethics and Pastoral Care.* Philadelphia: Fortress, 1983.

———. *Religious Thought and the Modern Psychologies.* Philadelphia: Fortress, 1987.

Brueggemann, Walter. *Hopeful Imagination: Prophetic Voices in Exile.* Philadelphia: Fortress, 1986.

Capps, Donald. "The Deadly Sins and Saving Virtues: How They Are Viewed by Clergy." *Pastoral Psychology* 40 (1992) 209–33.

———. "The Deadly Sins and Saving Virtues: How They Are Viewed By Laity." *Pastoral Psychology* 37 (1989) 229–53.

———. *Pastoral Care: A Thematic Approach.* Philadelphia: Westminster, 1979.

Carr, David. *Educating the Virtues: An Essay on the Philosophical Psychology of Moral Development and Education.* New York and London: Routledge, 1991.

Cherry, Conrad. *The Theology of Jonathan Edwards: A Reappraisal.* Bloomington and Indianapolis: Indiana University Press, 1990.

Couture, Pamela D., and Rodney J. Hunter. *Pastoral Care and Social Conflict.* Nashville: Abingdon, 1995.

Davidson, Edward H. "From Locke to Edwards." *Journal of the History of Ideas* 24 (1963) 355–72.

———. *Jonathan Edwards. The Narrative of a Puritan Mind.* Boston: Houghton Mifflin, 1966.

Donahue, James A. "The Use of Virtue and Character in Applied Ethics." *Horizons* 17 (1990) 228–43.

French, Peter A., Theodore E. Uehling, and Howard K. Wettstein. *Midwest Studies in Philosophy. XIII. Ethical Theory: Character and Virtue.* Notre Dame, IN: University of Notre Dame Press, 1988.

Furman, Ben, and Tapani Ahola. *Solution Talk: Hosting Therapeutic Conversations.* New York: Norton, 1992.

Geach, P. T. *The Virtues*. New York: Cambridge University Press, 1977.
Gerstner, John H. G. *Jonathan Edwards: A Mini-Theology*. Wheaton, IL: Tyndale, 1987.
———. *The Rational Biblical Theology of Jonathan Edwards*, vol. 1. Powhatan, VA: Berea, 1991.
Gutierrez, Gustavo. *A Theology of Liberation*. Maryknoll, NY: Orbis, 1988.
Gustafson, James M. *Theology and Christian Ethics*. Philadelphia: United Church Press, 1974.
Hauerwas, Stanley. *Character and the Christian Life: A Study in Theological Ethics*. San Antonio, TX: Trinity University Press, 1975.
———. *A Community of Character: Toward a Constructive Christian Social Ethic*. Notre Dame, IN: University of Notre Dame Press, 1981.
———. *Vision and Virtue*. Notre Dame, IN: Fides, 1974.
Hauerwas, Stanley, and Alasdair MacIntyre. *Revisions: Changing Perspectives in Moral Philosophy*. Notre Dame, IN: University of Notre Dame Press, 1983.
Heyns, L. M., and H. J. C. Pieterse. *A Primer in Practical Theology*. Menlo Park, Pretoria: Gnosis Books, 1990.
Hiltner, Seward. "Pastoral Psychology and Pastoral Counseling." *Pastoral Psychology* 3 (1952) 21–28.
———. *Preface to Pastoral Theology*. Nashville: Abingdon, 1958.
Hunter, Rodney J. *Dictionary of Pastoral Care and Counseling*. Nashville: Abingdon, 1990.
Jenson, Robert W. *America's Theologian: A Recommendation of Jonathan Edwards*. Oxford: Oxford University Press, 1988.
Johnston, Thomas H., and Clarence H. Faust. *Jonathan Edwards: Representative Selections*. Revised ed. New York: Hill and Wang, 1962.
Jones, L. Gregory. "Alasdair MacIntyre on Narrative, Community, and the Moral Life." *Modern Theology* 4 (1987) 53–69.
Kemp, Charles F. "The Pastoral Care Movement: A Product of Many Contributions." *Pastoral Psychology* 18 (1967) 29–44.
Kierkegaard, Soren. *The Sickness unto Death: A Christian Psychological Exposition for Upbuilding and Awakening*. 1849. Translated by Edna and Howard Long. Princeton, NJ: Princeton University Press, 1980.
Lapsley, James N. "On Defining Pastoral Theology." *Journal of Pastoral Theology* 1 (1991) 116–24.
Lauritzen, Paul. "Emotions and Religious Ethics." *The Journal of Religious Ethics* 16 (1988) 307–24.
Lyttle, David. "The Sixth Sense of Jonathan Edwards." *Church Quarterly Review* 167 (1966) 50–59.
Messer, Donald E. *Contemporary Images of Christian Ministry*. Nashville: Abingdon, 1989.
Milbank, John. *The Word Made Strange: Theology, Language, Culture*. Oxford: Blackwell, 1997.
Miller, Perry. *Jonathan Edwards*. 1949. Reprint, Amherst, MA: The University of Massachusetts Press, 1981.
———. "Jonathan Edwards on the Sense of the Heart." *Harvard Theological Review* 41 (1948) 123–45.
Neuhaus, Richard John. *Freedom for Ministry*. 1979. Reprint, Grand Rapids: Eerdmans, 1992.

———. *Virtue—Public and Private*. Grand Rapids: Eerdmans, 1986.
Niebuhr, Reinhold. *An Interpretation of Christian Ethics*. 1935. Reprint, San Francisco: Harper & Row, 1963.
Nouwen, Henri J. M., Donald P. McNeill, and Douglas A. Morrison. *Compassion: A Reflection on the Christian Life*. Garden City, NY: Doubleday, 1983.
Oates, Wayne E. *The Christian Pastor*. Philadelphia: Westminster, 1982.
———. *Pastoral Counseling*. Philadelphia: Westminster, 1974.
Oden, Thomas C. *Pastoral Theology: Essentials of Ministry*. San Francisco: Harper & Row, 1983.
Oglesby, William B. Jr. "Present Status and Future Prospects in Pastoral Theology." *Pastoral Psychology* 29 (1980) 36–45.
Peacock, Virginia A. *Problems in the Interpretation of Jonathan Edwards' The Nature of True Virtue*. Queenston, ON: Edwin Mellen, 1990.
Putnam, Ruth Anna. "Reciprocity and Virtue Ethics." *Ethics* 98 (1988) 379–89.
Sapp, Gary L. *Compassionate Ministry*. Birmingham, AL: Religious Education Press, 1980.
Scharfenberg, Joachim. *Pastoral Care as Dialogue*. Translated by O. C. Dean Jr. Philadelphia: Fortress, 1980.
Scheick, William J., ed. *Critical Essays on Jonathan Edwards*. Boston: Hall, 1980.
Schneedwind, J. B. "The Misfortunes of Virtue." *Ethics* 101 (1990) 42–63.
Smith, Claude A. "Jonathan Edwards and 'The Way of Ideas.'" *Harvard Theological Review* 59 (1966) 153–73.
Smith, Robert Doyle. "John Wesley and Jonathan Edwards on Religious Experience: A Comparative Analysis." *Wesleyan Theological Journal* 25:1 (1990) 130–46.
Spohn, William C. "The Return of Virtue Ethics." *Theological Studies* 53 (1992) 60–75.
———. "Sovereign Beauty: Jonathan Edwards and the Nature of True Virtue." *Theological Studies* 42 (1981) 394–421.
Tidball, Derek. *Skillful Shepherds: An Introduction to Pastoral Theology*. Grand Rapids: Zondervan, 1986.
Turnbull, Ralph G. *Jonathan Edwards: The Preacher*. Grand Rapids: Baker, 1958.
Wainwright, William. "Jonathan Edwards and the Sense of the Heart." *Faith and Philosophy* 7 (1990) 43–62.
Way, Peggy Ann. "Pastoral Excellence and Pastoral Theology: A Slight Shift of Paradigm and a Modest Polemic." *Pastoral Psychology* 29 (1980) 46–57.
Weil, Simone. *Lectures on Philosophy*. Cambridge: Cambridge University Press, 1978.
Woggon, Frank Milstead. "Deliberate Activity as an Art for (Almost) Everyone: Friedrich Schleiermacher on Practical Theology." *Journal of Pastoral Care* 48 (1994) 3–13.
Yearly, Lee H. "Recent Work on Virtue." *Religious Studies Review* 16 (1990) 1–9.

Index

Alderman, H., 54–55
Alves, R. A., 82–84, 113–14, 128
Aristotle, 47, 69
Aquinas, 59, 70

Berger, P. L., 34–36
Boisen, A., 5, 88, 95, 117
Bonhoeffer, D., 103, 110, 117
Brockelman, P. T., 95
Browning, D. S., 103–5, 111
Brueggemann, W., 82
Burck, J. R., 3
Byrnes, T. A., 57–58

Campbell, A. V., 124–25
Capps, D., 84–87, 92, 94, 99, 115, 118, 124–26
Cessario, R., 53
Cone, J., 123
Conly, S., 46

Delattre, R. A., 17, 18, 63, 64, 66, 68, 69, 71, 73, 116, 125
Dwight, S. E., 23, 28

Edwards, J.
  Diary, 15
  Discourses, 17
  End of Creation, 17, 32
  Faithful Narrative, 11, 24, 25
  Farewell Sermon, 31–33, 37–38
  Freedom of the Will, 13, 32
  God Glorified in Man's Dependence, 22
  Humble Inquiry (Qualifications for Communion), 31–32
  Justification by Faith Alone, 23
  Memoirs, 12, 14, 16, 18, 19
  Notes on the Mind, 13
  Original Sin, 32
  Personal Narrative, 14–15
  Religious Affections, 11, 40–43, 72
  Resolutions, 19–21
  Sinners in the Hands of an Angry God, 28, 56
  True Excellency of a Gospel Minister, 39–40
  True Virtue, passim, esp. ch. 2
Erikson, J. M., 101

Farley, B. W., 59
Fiddes, P. S., 75, 76
Fisch, R., 86, 87
Ford, S. D., 77, 97–101, 108, 121

Gilligan, C., 94, 95
Gutierrez, G., 117, 128

Haring, B., 115
Holbrook, C. A., 63
Hulme, W. E., 114
Hunter, R. J., 3, 104–6, 111, 112, 113, 116, 118, 120, 122, 124, 126

Jennings, T. W., Jr., 2, 3
Jones, D. C., 47

Kotva, J. J., 47–50, 55
Kreeft, P., 53, 89, 118

Langan, J. P., 53
Lee, S. H., 10, 13, 57, 63, 64, 65, 67
Levan, C., 93
Loder, J. E., 91

MacIntyre, A., 47, 49, 50, 57, 58, 127
Meilaender, G. C., 2, 51, 53
Merleau–Ponty, M., 95, 96
Miller, P., 13, 37
Moltmann, J., 89–91, 121–22
Murdoch, I., 52
Murray, I. H., 12, 13, 15, 19, 28

Niebuhr, H. R., 58
Niebuhr, R. R., 66
Nouwen, H. J. M., 80, 114, 118, 119, 120

Patton, J., 95, 96, 122
Peterson, E. H., 96, 99
Proudfoot, W., 72

Ramsey, P., 2, 17, 57, 63, 65, 67
Rilke, R. M., 82
Rogers, C., 119
Romero, O., 97
Rorty, A. O., 53–55

Simonson, H. P., 63
Soelle, D., 80–81, 115, 123
Solomon, D., 46, 49–52
Statman, D., 47, 50, 52, 54
SteinhoffSmith, R., 123
Stone, B. P., 121

Tillich, P., 77–79, 87, 91, 92, 114, 116, 119

Wallace, J. D., 46, 48
Watzlawick, Paul, 86, 87
Weakland, J., 86, 87
Weil, S., 77, 93, 114
Westra, H. P., 36–41
Whitehead, A. N., 66, 67
Wilcox, M. W., 94
Winslow, O., 22–25, 29, 31